Y0-BZF-544

PORTFOLIO

INNOVATE HAPPILY

Dr Rekha Shetty, PhD is the founder of the MindsPower brand and managing director of Farstar Distribution Network Ltd, a twenty-year-old consulting firm working exclusively on innovation initiatives, happiness and work–life balance. She consults for some of the region's foremost blue-chip companies and is keenly involved in social action for clean water and population development issues. She is one of the first women Rotary International governors in Asia and a recipient of Rotary's 'Service above Self' award. Her other books include *The Way to a Healthy Heart: The Zero Heart Attack Path*; *Portable Roots, Corporate Strategy: Mindspower Innovation*; *Innovate! 90 Days to Transform Your Business* and *The Happiness Quotient*. Dr Rekha Shetty's thoughts come from a deep study of many disciplines including management, sociology, psychology, economics, history and spirituality. Her ideas are practised in over thirty countries.

You can get in touch with Dr Rekha Shetty at rekhashetty123@gmail.com or rekhasmindspower@airtelmail.in. You can also visit her blogs http://innovation90days.blogspot.com and http://thehappinessquotient123.blogspot.com, and join http://www.facebook.com/authorrekhashetty.

Innovate Happily!

A Blueprint for Shangri-La, the High Happiness Quotient City

DR REKHA SHETTY, PH D

PORTFOLIO
PENGUIN

PORTFOLIO
Published by the Penguin Group
Penguin Books India Pvt. Ltd, 11 Community Centre, Panchsheel Park,
New Delhi 110 017, India
Penguin Group (USA) Inc., 375 Hudson Street, New York, New York
10014, USA
Penguin Group (Canada), 90 Eglinton Avenue East, Suite 700, Toronto,
Ontario, M4P 2Y3, Canada (a division of Pearson Penguin Canada Inc.)
Penguin Books Ltd, 80 Strand, London WC2R 0RL, England
Penguin Ireland, 25 St Stephen's Green, Dublin 2, Ireland (a division of
Penguin Books Ltd)
Penguin Group (Australia), 250 Camberwell Road, Camberwell,
Victoria 3124, Australia (a division of Pearson Australia Group Pty Ltd)
Penguin Group (NZ), 67 Apollo Drive, Rosedale, Auckland 0632,
New Zealand (a division of Pearson New Zealand Ltd)
Penguin Group (South Africa) (Pty) Ltd, 24 Sturdee Avenue, Rosebank,
Johannesburg 2196, South Africa

Penguin Books Ltd, Registered Offices: 80 Strand, London WC2R 0RL, England

First published in Portfolio by Penguin Books India 2012
Copyright © Dr Rekha Shetty 2012

ISBN 9780143418542

Typeset in Sabon by Guru Typograph Technology, New Delhi
Printed at Thomson Press India Ltd, New Delhi

Beyond Certainty

Come,
Where the imagination floats free—
A butterfly in the wind

Listen,
Beyond the certainty of words
And hear the symphony
Of a seashell in your ear

See,
Beyond the known
And fly a thousand leagues
Into the heart of a sun-drenched flower

Forsake
The certainty of black and white
For the shadowed grey.

Prologue

There is a place in the distant mountains which is always calm and peaceful, where the earth is laden with luscious fruit and wholesome grain, where people are vibrant, healthy and happy, where every edifice is artistic and beauty clothes every home in the loveliness of handmade artifacts. Lush greenery carpets the land, dazzling your eyes with its colourful butterflies, exotic animals and birds. The air is fresh and the water is pure and the sound of holy mantras is carried on every gentle breeze. Here the whole community is a family and smiles bind the hearts of all. You too can live in Shangri-La . . .

one

The first time I met him was in a bar. He was thoughtfully sipping a lime drink that might have contained vodka, gin or simply lime juice. What drew me to him was the quiet island of reflective silence he had created in the midst of the noise and the smoke.

'I like the energy of this place,' he said, smiling at me. The open, joyful smile decided it for me—I took the high stool next to him. 'I came here to drink myself into a stupor,' I said. He responded with a gesture that said, 'Be my guest.' I ordered a large whisky on the rocks and started my trip into oblivion.

'So what happened?' he asked quietly.

'It's my boss BB,' I said. I wished I could describe my first, fire-breathing, macho boss.

'Well, he's the type who wears barbed wire next to his skin and eats broken bottles for breakfast,' I said.

'So you like P.G. Wodehouse too,' he laughed. 'That was Aunt Agatha, I believe.'

I tried to recreate for him the daily demolition of my ego that happened at the morning meetings at office, leaving me drained of all energy.

'Hey, by the way, my name is Raghav. My friends call me Rags.' My hand was engulfed in a warm handshake.

'I am Arjun . . . my friends call me Junie.'

We sipped our drinks meditatively for a while.

'What do you like or admire about your boss?' he asked.

I looked at him aghast. Something good about that fire-breathing dragon! That gorgon whose glance could turn me into stone?

'Stop being dramatic!' said Raghav, responding to my thoughts as though it were the most natural thing in the world for him to hear my unspoken thoughts.

'Well, he knows a lot. He should—since, as he says, his experience is more than my age.'

'How old are you? Twenty-eight?' he asked.

'Yes,' I nodded.

He looked affectionately at me like I was his little brother. I had never had an elder brother and quite liked the feeling.

'Maybe your boss would like to feel that you admire him.'

I gave him a scornful, disbelieving look.

'If you look at him like that, every line of your face shows your utter and total disregard for him,' he said. I hadn't realized my feelings were so transparently displayed on my face.

'Why don't you leave?' he asked.

'I can't leave two months after joining. It will look bad on my CV.'

'Okay—why don't you somehow express your respect for his knowledge and experience tomorrow? Everyone longs for affirmation. Your boss is not getting it from you.'

'He can also say something good about me. I was a college topper in business school. I was also captain of the football team.'

'You start the process and see what happens. It is a cycle that only the victim can start.'

I looked at him disbelievingly. Suddenly, I didn't feel like continuing my binge any more. I ordered a 'cricket' lime drink, and chatted about how it was to be in this brand new city: Chennai. It was strange, so different from my hometown, Patna, from Bihar, from IIT Kharagpur and IIM Bangalore. I really missed the easy affection of my friends at the Institute.

'Everything changes,' he said. 'Either you can be a victim of change or you can proactively create a tidal wave of change.'

I goggled at him. 'Who are you? Michael Porter?' I scoffed.

'Just call me Rags,' he said lightly.

And when I turned back after downing my drink he was gone.

No telephone number, no address, nothing.

Monday morning. Black Monday. One more day under the dark cloud of disregard that enveloped the review meetings.

'So what does young Kotler have to say about our new product launch in Libya?'

My head jerked up from my aimless doodling as BB's voice pierced the silence. He was talking to me. At his sarcastic best.

I struggled to keep quiet. Not willing to play his vicious cat and mouse game any more. The meeting moved into the structured and disciplined format where all participants presented their points of view. In spite of myself, I was impressed by the precise, focussed decision making process. Many decisions were made by BB, but he certainly made sure he had all the facts first.

When my turn came to present ideas for the advertising

campaign, I suddenly felt Rags's voice in my head. 'Give him an affirmation.'

'This meeting and the presentations I have heard have given me a much clearer perspective for the proposed campaign,' I said. 'I would like to rework the campaign with some ideas heard here. Here are a few ideas which all of you can think about and mail me.'

There was a stunned silence; you could have heard a pin drop. Everyone was staring at me.

'Okay,' said BB, looking at me speculatively. Like, 'Maybe he is not as dumb as he looks. Maybe he can still listen to others and learn and stop acting like a hotshot brat.'

I tried to process what was happening. Rima, the cute product executive who usually minuted the meetings, grinned at me. 'So, even you have something good to say about us.'

Did I really seem like such an insufferable know-it-all? I had to know. So when I found Rima sitting over a cup of coffee in the canteen, I flopped down beside her and asked, 'Am I so bad?'

'No, you fool,' she said, smiling sweetly. 'You are worse. With all your graphs and slick presentations that don't mean anything to these guys who have their brains fried in the hot, noisy factory every day.'

I looked at her, chastened, and thought how lovely she looked, so intense and sincere.

I walked off with a vague wave. I looked at the messages on my cell phone. There was a message from an unknown number.

Ur ok

How did Rags know my phone number?

The year passed. And then another. My rough edges were smoothed out. My rise was described by some as meteoric. I had a great team which I led as Branch Head, I had a new car, lots of Saturday night friends, a neat pad. Life was good.

One day I was at the Hilton Hyatt Regency bar. I really enjoyed watching Naveen Fernandez juggling a dozen bottles in the air and miraculously pouring out the vodka from a bottle tucked neatly under his arm. Not once did he drop any of the dozen things he was juggling. I wished I could juggle the dozen priorities in my life as a branch manager. Some things would bounce back like the rubber ball he suddenly dropped, to add to the excitement. I imagined myself juggling the urgent and the important. My work, family, health, friends and myself. Some of those bottles could easily break. The last two years I had been mindful of that.

Suddenly my cell phone rang. 'Hey,' said the unforgettable voice, so familiar even after all those months.

'Rags!' I cried. 'Where are you?'

'Just passing through, I heard you've got your promotion and become Branch Manager. So you got everything you wanted.' I could almost see his smile. He was teasing me as usual.

'Rags . . .' I said.

'Junie, I was wondering whether you would like to take a trip to Bhutan, the land of the Gross National Happiness, and play ping-pong with a few ideas on innovation.'

'What . . .?'

'Innovation is the most blissful thing you can do . . . Do you want to come?'

'Yes, but . . .'

'On 15 October. Just for a month. We can see Bhutan, too.'

On the spot, I decided to go. And after that, things moved really fast.

two

Taxiing into Paro airport, between mist-wreathed mountains and green valleys, seemed impossibly dream-like. It is a magical place, amidst gentle, undulating, grey-green mountains, where nature and man conspire to create an image of infinite beauty. Rich, terraced farmlands stretch into the horizon. Far away, I could see the snow-clad Mount Jhomolahari (7000 metres high). The glaciers on its distant mountain slopes melt to plunge down through deep gorges, resulting in a serpentine river: Pa-chu. The airport building intricately painted with the eight lucky signs looked like something out of the lost land of Shangri-La, with pagoda-like sloping roofs, wooden beams, painted columns. I was bedazzled, enchanted. The words of a poem skipped through my mind.

Joy

My mind
Racing through the misty mountains at dawn
Scattering my thoughts
On the sands of Time
Like prodigal children
Leaping over silver puddles
Of rain

As I walked out of the airport, I saw Rags standing there, decked in shorts and a large colourful hat. My eyes filled with tears at the sight of him. I laughed and cried simultaneously as we thumped each other on the back.

'How did you get here?' I asked.

'Walked here of course: I am not a Branch Head and have a lot of time,' he retorted.

Over delicious noodle soup in a little shack, we talked of everything and nothing, laughing like school kids out on an unexpected holiday. 'So this is Bhutan, Land of the Thunder Dragon, in the mid-Himalayas. Just 600,000 people,' I said, looking around.

Our driver Kandu was a bouncing, twinkling Bhutanese dressed in a traditional woven blue Gho (a comfortable garment resembling a Scottish kilt, worn with socks, with the knees showing). He had taught himself English and embodied the slogan of 'Happiness starts with a smile'. Yeshay, our guide, would join us the next day. His child was ill and had to be hospitalized in a distant village.

'So how is India Inc's youngest BM feeling? What are you now? Thirty? And not bad, no paunch to speak of . . .' Rags looked me up and down.

'Thanks to you and your e-mails on exercising from the tips of my toes to the top of my head,' I said. 'As for this youngest BM business, I am not sure for how long . . .'

'So bad?' he asked, suddenly sombre.

'Worse,' I said. 'The global downturn—'

As we walked to our hotel, I told him everything. The plummeting revenues, the piling inventory, the rising costs, the dissatisfied customers, the discontented employees.

In the courtyard of the riverside resort which has the river Pa-chu flowing through it, I stopped transfixed as I saw a juggler juggling a dozen balls. I floated into an unsettled feeling of déjà vu. I looked at Rags, who was smiling placidly as he said, 'Feel like that, do you?'

I nodded helplessly.

'Think of those balls as men, materials, machines, methods, markets and money—the 6 Ms,' he said. 'Once you learn to handle them innovatively, you will be able to beat the downturn.'

We walked into our rooms. I looked across at Rags's room just in time to see him spreading his blanket on the floor to settle down beside the pristine bed. He waved and called out, 'The floor is better for the back. You should try it sometime.'

I looked out of my window at the bubbling river, the mountains that were so close by. It was like being transported back to the 1930s James Hilton classic *The Lost Horizon*. The High Lama who is charged with protecting the people, culture and tradition from being corrupted by 'outside' influences says in *The Lost Horizon*, 'We may expect no mercy, but we may faintly hope for neglect. Here we shall stay with our books and our music and our meditations, covering the frail elegances of a dying age, and seeking such wisdom as men will need when their passions are all spent. We have a heritage to cherish and bequeath. Let us take what pleasure we may, until that time comes.' James Hilton is said to have written *The Lost Horizon* with Bhutan in mind.

'In Bhutan one often feels that time has stood still,' says my guidebook.

'Bhutan has a Commission on Gross National Happiness which was involved in reducing the defence budget and spending more on education and health. The theme seems to be "Less cars, more stars"', says Rags. 'The more you want, the more you struggle. You have to decide how much of yourself you want to give up, to have more.'

'Psychologist Martin Seligman provides the acronym PERMA to summarize positive psychology's correlational findings,' he continued. 'Human beings seem to be the happiest when they have:

1. Pleasure (tasty foods, warm baths etc.)
2. Engagement (or flow, the absorption of an enjoyed yet challenging activity)
3. Relationships (social ties have turned out to be extremely reliable indicators of happiness)
4. Meaning (a perceived quest or belonging to something bigger), and
5. Accomplishments (having realized tangible goals)

Spending money on others actually makes us happier than spending it on ourselves,' Rags finished.

Some hours drifted by. 'Let us look at this ying-yang tool,' said Rags jokingly, fresh from his nap.

**

6M Positives and Negatives

The 6M is a template and a blueprint to think ideas through. It can be used with every tool and helps teams to separate the positive from the negative.

Each of the six key elements of a business can be analysed, identifying the feelings of all stakeholders.

For example, invite all employees to write on post-it slips what the pluses and the minuses in the company are as per the following table:

6M	Positive (+)	Negative (−)
Men		
Materials		
Machines		
Methods		
Markets		
Money		

'Do not be afraid to ask questions even if it makes you look ignorant—nobody is expected to know everything,' Rags said. 'The purpose of this trip is to understand how to create happy communities and countries. John Adams wrote about the greatest "quantity" of human happiness. The special challenge will be to give people innovative thinking tools to create happy communities.'

'You mean formulae which can help us to find "out of the box" ideas and solve problems and create new processes?'

'Yes. Each community has its own unique problems and solutions. So we need to arm the people with thinking tools. Then they can think through their own problems. There is no use trying to impose our ideas on them. No one will implement them then.'

'Happy communities can happen only when people stop being selfish and start working together to solve everyone's problems,' I said.

'*Vasudeva kutumbam*, or the whole world is one family. So let us start looking at our own small area.'

'Chennai, where I live,' said I.

'Fine,' said Rags.

I was thrilled to be part of this plan. 'As we travel, let us develop a strategy to create a happy city,' I said.

'You strategize. I plan to enjoy myself,' said Rags, running up the slope.

In my hand was a rainbow-coloured folder which said 'Shangri-La'.

* *

Shangri-La

Since the beginning of time, mankind has been looking for a fabled land where you can always be happy and remain young forever. They gave it many names.

In every case this dream land is cut off from the real world, protected from outside influences and the people there lead simple, natural, pastoral lives. The Garden of Eden, to which no one can return, is the earliest image. We lost our keys to Eden due to our loss of innocence, our knowledge of good and evil and the sin of disobedience.

And there is Atlantis, the paradise which Plato describes, 'which sank into the ocean in a single day and night of misfortune'.

Avalon, a Welsh island where Excalibur, the mythical sword of King Arthur, was forged. King Arthur is taken there, so that his fatal wounds could be healed.

Xanadu, a dream garden.

El Dorado, a mythical city paved with gold.

Tocharian Tushara, a mythical kingdom in the Mahabharata.

Agharta, Hyberborea, Iram of the Pillars, Thule, Utopia, the Fountain of Youth. The list is endless.

This journey is the search for knowledge, knowing how to create this happy town, city, and finally, this nation. It is a search carried out in Bhutan, the land that gave the world the term Gross National Happiness. Bhutan is being described as the world's last Shangri-La. Described in James Hilton's classic work *The Lost Horizon*, it gives us a glimpse of such places which were meant to be sanctuaries for human civilization:

> As he stared at that superb mountain, he felt a glow of satisfaction that there were such places still left on earth, distant, inaccessible, as yet 'unhumanised'. The icy ramparts were now more striking than ever against the northern sky, which had become mouse-coloured and sinister. The peaks had a chill gleam; utterly majestic and remote, their very namelessness had dignity.

He also foresaw a time when men, exultant in the technique of homicide, would rage so hotly over the world that every precious thing would be in danger, every book and picture and harmony, every treasure garnered through two millennia, the small, the delicate, the defenceless—all would be lost like the lost books of Livy, or wrecked as the English wrecked the summer palace in Peking.

It will be such a war, as the world has not seen before. There will be no safety by arms, no help from authority, no answer in science. It will rage until every flower of culture is trampled, and all human things are levelled in vast chaos.

But the Dark Ages that are to come will cover the whole world in a single pall; there will be neither escape nor sanctuary, save such as are too secret to be found or too humble to be noticed. And Shangri-La may hope to be both of these.

**

I closed the folder.

My first view of Bhutan gave me that same slow, silent, calm feeling one has on hearing great classical music. But today, is it possible to protect any country like Bhutan, which has access to forty-five TV channels? What about the revolution of rising expectations that spawns the discos in Thimpu as well as brings the news of the world into every drawing room?

Guarded by mountain walls, this dream place of endless happiness, where people remained young forever—can it exist in the twenty-first century? Like a colourful coral that is leached of colour and life when it is taken out of the ocean, those who live there fall into death and decay as soon as they leave.

'Health care is free in Bhutan,' Rags said. 'A medical college is being built, but so far most of the doctors have been trained in India. Their traditional method Sow Rigpa promotes positive health, like our own Ayurveda. The practice of yoga and pranayama is intrinsic to both cultures. Here a thinking tool called Turn It Upside Down can be used to promote health, wellness and well-being, rather than waiting to treat sickness after it strikes. More health preservation centres must be created. Children should study the science of life and well-being as part of their school syllabus. At a fraction of the cost the nation can have health as the prime mover of progress.'

Next morning I was religiously doing my exercises, when Rags called me from the courtyard that featured a fountain, impossibly colourful flowers and chirping birds. 'Come down fast, before they run out of breakfast,' he said.

I came down just in time. Rags lovingly watched me eating, the way my mother used to, absently throwing a few crumbs to a cat with topaz eyes that had curled up at his feet.

Suddenly he picked up an ice cube from the porcelain dish and put it into my hand. 'Hold it,' he said.

'Till when?' I asked.

'As long as you can.'

My hand felt numb. I never knew that ice could be so cold. After several minutes, I said, 'It's melted.'

'An ice cube is not an ice cube forever,' Rags said. 'Ice melts and becomes water, with the touch of sunlight it evaporates and becomes air. And air knows the freedom of the skies. Nothing can hold air captive.'

I looked at him.

'That is the first law of Innovation,' he said. 'Everything changes. You have come to the right place to learn about impermanence—to Bhutan where the Buddha's teachings created a code for living. The core value is that nothing in the world is permanent or lasting. Everything is changing, momentary and unpredictable. Bhutan is the only Vajrayana Buddhist nation in the world today, and the profound teachings of this tradition remain well preserved and exert a strong influence in all aspects of life here.'

Rags made complex ideas sound so simple.

I often felt like Alice in Wonderland: running faster and faster to stay in the same place. But the world was moving so fast, the pace of change was so rapid that standing still for even a moment meant falling behind.

'Don't become a victim of hurry sickness,' said Rags. 'Wait till the soul catches up with your body. Take time to reflect instead of rushing mindlessly in the wrong direction.'

He handed over a neat rainbow-coloured booklet.

**

Everything Changes

This is the first of the Laws of Innovation. Everything changes: people, products, companies; Men, Materials, Machines, Methods, Markets and Money (the 6Ms). The decision to change is in your hands.

Innovation is about transformation. Imagine a block of ice. It is cold solid and transparent. But it is not a block of ice forever. It melts and flows across boundaries. Water follows its own logic which is very different from the logic of ice. Water goes to many places, has many adventures, but always comes back to its own nature: cool, beautiful and still. If you heat it, it boils; keep heating, it becomes part of the air by becoming steam, steam that knows the freedom of the skies, steam that cannot be held captive. Add pressure and it can rotate turbines to generate power.

Transformation is what happens to a drop of water when it is touched by the magic of sunlight. It becomes a rainbow. It is what happens to a seed when it starts the journey to become a mighty banyan tree. The banyan tree is not an improved seed, just as a butterfly is not an improved caterpillar or a rainbow an improved drop of water. By definition, innovation is taking interesting ideas and transforming them into usable solutions for business problems.

**

'The key is to understand the fact that everything can be proactively changed. Apply the idea of the 6Ms to your problem,' Rags challenged me.

16

'Look at this brick,' he said, handing me a bright red one left over from a recent construction. 'Apply the same principle to the brick.'

'Huh . . . what?'

'Apply the principle of the ice cube to the brick. A brick is not a brick forever.'

'So what is it?'

'It can become a building, a wall. It can stop a door from banging shut . . .'

'Wait! It can be powdered and used for a rangoli design!' I cried out.

'Wow! That's the first breakthrough thought. Once you can let go of your obsession with the brick with its rectangular shape, then you can really do things with it.'

'Like add water to the brick dust and mould it into a tortoise?'

'Okay, you got the idea. You can go back and look at the principle as it applies to the 6Ms which form the actual skeleton of a company, a home, a country.

Remember that all the 6Ms are subject to change. Of course they will change on their own, due to the maya of time. But you can also proactively change each of them by consistent effort.'

'We can do it! Together we can! Like Obama said,' I laughed.

'Or change! Change! Like the conductor on a bus always says!' came Rags's rejoinder. We doubled up with laughter.

Walking past us were a school of monks in red robes. The oldest of them glanced at us with a pained expression.

'How come you don't wear saffron or a monk's gown?' I asked.

Rags was suddenly serious. 'I have a horror of being a magnet for followers who want a piece of me. I do not want the bondage of an administration, dealing with millions of bucks and fighting over it! I feel if I stay in one place for too long, people and activities will grow around me like clinging creepers. For peace of mind, resign as general manager of the Universe—that's a Larry Eisenberg quote, he was CEO of Disney.'

'How and why are you spending so much time with me?' I asked, bewildered.

He looked at me reflectively. 'Everything, every great, good change has happened because of the sustained effort of one pure, high-minded individual . . . Maybe you could be that person, that catalyst.'

I was dumbstruck.

'Think about my idea,' he said. 'All leaders, national and corporate and local community leaders should be trained to think innovatively; first by learning the 47 thinking tools and second by installing the positive field which will increase the Happiness Quotient of the company, the community or the country. Every day, each of us should work to make things better, so that we become a nation of problem solvers rather than a country of problem creators.'

My jaw dropped as I realized the magnitude of what he was saying. This was about making India a great nation with the culture of innovation. Was he about to take over my life?

At the end of my present path I could be a head honcho of India Inc. Was this what I really wanted? Would my life be a life of significance? Would this journey give me a feeling of having mattered?

Rags handed me a post-it slip. It said:

Time stood still, my breathing had become slow and steady. Rags called my name gently and I opened my eyes, to find him standing near me. 'Namaste means, I bow to the divine in you,' said Rags. 'The Vedas tell us that the divine spark dwells in all. This means that the divine exists within each of us. One does not have to evolve into a divine being. One already is. You just have to get rid of what is not divine. In the Taithriya Upanishad, the son asks Varuna about the nature of Brahman. Varuna helps his son realize that it is not food, breath, mind, wisdom or bliss. All these are but sheaths enveloping the immortal Self.'

I silently absorbed this knowledge.

'How do you explain sweetness to a child? He has to eat sugar and understand what it is. So too each person has to find the Self and taste it himself.' Rags was trying to bridge the gap with words. But words are not the right vehicle to communicate the nuances of the soul. Realization is an individual experience, exclusive and unique.

'The Buddhists teachers have *kagyu* or whispered communication, breathing and postures, mantras and mudras,' explained Rags, 'but internalizing and understanding is

19

something that the student has to do for himself. This understanding comes as much from being with the teacher as it does from his words or actions.'

'Are you a guru?' I asked Rags.

Rags said, 'Life is the greatest guru. Learn from it. Get rid of what is not divine—just as one has to get rid of all the marble in a block that is not a statue. For those who see the divine radiance in the face of all, nurturing that radiance is the purpose of human life. To get rid of the spirit of separateness and seeing the unity of all is the purpose of many lifetimes.'

Rags gave me a parchment with a story told by the Buddha.

*

A Divine Vision

Once there lived a poor artist who left his home, leaving his wife, to seek his fortune. After three years of hard struggle he had saved three hundred pieces of gold and decided to return home. On his way he came to a great temple in which a grand ceremony of offering was in progress. He was greatly impressed by it and thought to himself: 'Hitherto, I have thought only of the present; I have never considered my future happiness. It is a part of my good fortune that I have come to this place; I must take advantage of it to plant seeds of merit.' Thinking thus, he gratefully donated all his savings to the temple and returned to his home penniless.

When he reached home, his wife reproached him for not bringing her some money. The poor artist replied that he had earned some money but had put it where it would be safe. When she pressed him to tell her where he had hidden it, he confessed that he had given it to the monks at a temple.

This made the wife angry and she scolded her husband and finally carried the matter to the local judge. When the judge asked the artist for his defence, the artist said that he had not acted foolishly, for he had earned the money after a long and hard struggle and wanted to use it as seed for future good fortune. When he came to the temple it seemed to him that there was the field where he should plant his gold as seed for good fortune. Then he added: 'When I gave the monks the gold, it seemed that I was throwing away all greed and stinginess from my mind, and I have realized that real wealth is not gold but your mind.'

The judge praised the artist's spirit, and those who heard of this manifested their approval by helping him in various ways. Thus the artist and his wife entered into permanent good fortune.

[from *The Teaching of Buddha—Bukkyo Dendo Kyokai*]

* *

I laughed and told Rags how the great Tamil poet Subramanya Bharathi fed the last handful of grain in his house to the sparrows. The grain was borrowed from a neighbour by his long-suffering wife.

Suddenly I felt someone tugging at my shirt. Right next to me was a white, fluffy, slightly bedraggled dog, looking expectantly at me. I put out a tentative hand and petted him. He leaned back with eyes shut and I scratched him behind his ears. He loved it. At the campfire on the river bank, he lay by my side all night. Somehow, he made me feel safe and comfortable.

We decided to call him Sirius after the brightest star in the sky, the Dog Star.

'Why are the stars so bright here and as large as chrysanthemums?' I asked.

'That's because the atmosphere is so clear and there is no smog like you have in Chennai,' said Rags.

'Chennai has far less smog than Mumbai, Delhi or Kolkata,' I said defensively.

'I am sure you are the only one responsible for that,' said Rags, grinning from ear to ear. I was too relaxed to even throw a pebble at him. I looked at Sirius who was watching both of us through his fringe of scraggly hair. He really needed a bath, I thought, as he scratched himself.

I was looking forward to a good lazy holiday. It looked like Rags had other plans, though. 'Study this Innovation process and map tonight and we will talk tomorrow,' he said.

Homework certainly does not fit in with my idea of a holiday. I fell into a dreamless sleep. Sirius concurred with my feelings wholeheartedly. When I woke up in the morning, I found that he had torn the map into tiny pieces and stamped on it for good measure.

*

The MindsPower Process Map

	Problem Statement	Ideas Generation	Incubation	Analysis	Implementation
			Actions		
People	Identify Action Teams	Train teams in Mindspower tools	Put ideas on whiteboard	Group presentation	Identify Action Teams
Policies & Practices	Assess exiting management practices	Define, document and gain approval for recommended problem statement	Define goals and impact 6M implementation requirements	Analysis solution and choose best solutions	Management systems implementation
Mind Space	Ice breaker: nurturing climate	Install positive Nava Rasas	Open Mood: problem to sub-conscious mind	Switch on analytical mind: 5W and 1H	Left brain: logical mind
Change Management	Identify top management support, stakeholder impact and design communication, and training requirements			Executive communication training, compliance	Implement communication training, compliance
			Outcome		
	Challenge identification, ensure strategic importance	List of ideas ensure top management support	Cost benefit analysis	Detailed implementation plan	Create linkages: performance and rewards

The Innovation Process

The greatest competitive advantage comes from out-innovating the competition. As Tom Peters put it, 'Add ten differentiations to every product or service every sixty days. Sounds impossible. Isn't it tough? It is. But what are the options? Your competitors are not sitting still.'

Innovation is the ultimate human resource which can ensure the competitive advantage of companies.

The process that leads to the moment of discovery, invention, creativity and innovation can be broken down into five parts:

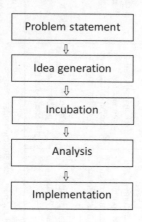

Problem Statement

Identifying and formulating the problem is the most difficult part of creative problem solving. Very often we state symptoms of the problems and end up wasting scarce resources chasing the illusionary 'golden deer' of the epics. Management then becomes so emotionally committed to the wrong path that we can end up moving faster and faster in the wrong direction. It is like a man who drills an oil well in a bad spot. More and more money is spent with no resulting oil strike. But those involved refuse to fill up the unproductive well and move on to a new location. They continue throwing good money after bad, because they do not want to admit that a mistake had been made initially.

Problem as first stated: How to improve the brakes supplied to the car maker?

Creative analysis: Why do we want to improve the brakes?

Answer: To stop cars at a shorter distance

Question: How else can we stop a car at a shorter distance?

Creative analysis: Why do we want to stop the car at a shorter distance?

Answer: To increase the safety of the occupants of the car

Restatement of problem: How might we improve safety in a car's stopping system?

Result: This is much broader than the original challenge and opens a wider door to novel ideas.

At one of my early creativity laboratories for mothers, twenty-five years ago, one of the participants said, 'My problem is: how do I get my son to eat eggs for breakfast?' A rigorous analysis of the problem uncovered the real quandary, 'How do I get my son to eat a nutritious breakfast?' The restatement of the problem enabled the mother to give the child a variety of foods ranging from cheese and idlis to cutlets and samosas, instead of forcing the child to eat the eggs, which he hated. Redefining the problem statement is the challenging part of the process, as all of us who have struggled with the task of arriving at a hypothesis, know.

The restatement of the problem opens up the possibility of tackling the mice menace through the use of gas, poison, biological methods and improved hygiene, instead of being fixated on improving the architecture of the mousetrap.

Problem: How to build a better mousetrap

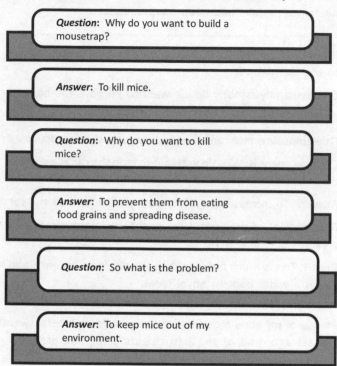

Question: Why do you want to build a mousetrap?

Answer: To kill mice.

Question: Why do you want to kill mice?

Answer: To prevent them from eating food grains and spreading disease.

Question: So what is the problem?

Answer: To keep mice out of my environment.

Thinking Tools for Idea Generation

My first major encounter with the power of a creative thinking tool was when, as senior manager of a hospital, I was faced with the challenge of marketing a hospital. There were no models in the Indian context. How does one market illness? The first hurdle encountered was what insurance people call the 'immortality complex'. Stated in simple terms the immortality complex postulates that all humans believe that they are immortal—they will never die or fall ill. It is only friends and the neighbours who will fall prey to such misfortune. It was then that we decided to use a favourite tool of mine—Turn it Upside Down (TUD).

The steps followed in TUD are:

- Normal belief: A hospital is a place for sick people.
- TUD: A hospital is a place for people who are healthy.

When we looked at a hospital as a place for people who are healthy:

1. Our base of customers increased to include a vast number of healthy people who come for positive health programmes. The positive health theme included the 'Well Woman' programme, which involved a health and beauty focus: yoga experts, beauticians, and women's health practitioners helped create a vastly successful programme. Preventive health care became a positive activity. Fifteen check-ups including the heart check, the diabetic check and the child health check were part of the wellness check portfolio.
2 The relationship with customers, which traditionally started on a note of pain, anxiety and death, began on a happy note. The focus was on how to remain healthy and how to face problems. The lifetime relationship, which is the bedrock of direct marketing today, started on a happy, positive note, with wellness as the key.

The MindsPower Innovation Toolkit has 47 Thinking Tools.

MindsPower Tools are particularly useful in cultures where one is taught to defer to elders. A tool enables you to disagree without being disagreeable. It also helps you to work around a disagreement like water finding its way around a stone. People are usually predominantly analytical or predominantly intuitive. They are either what is popularly called left-brained—logical, mathematical and statistical—or right-brained—intuitive, poetic and holistic.

The first type like everything clearly defined and are practical, wanting quick, clear solutions. All obstacles should be defined and solved up front for them. They prefer tried and tested methods. They do not want to generate alternatives that may be wasteful. They like boundaries to be defined even before they start. Innovation tools help them access their right brain.

The tools also help the intuitive types to access their left brain. It is the birthright of all humans to use all parts of their brain.

Thinking tools make the teaching of creativity simple. Tools can help us replicate innovation quickly across the organization. The world's foremost companies have insisted on teaching creativity and innovation skills. IBM, Coca-Cola, Unilever, Sony, ICICI, Ashok Leyland, TI, HLL, TVS—the list goes on. IBM even has a two-year innovation programme for all its engineers. MindsPower I-Labs, over the last twenty years, has been dedicated to improving the creative potential of Asian companies.

Indian companies have an opportunity to learn a shared language of Innovation Tools. It is only through the systematic learning of tools, the generation and testing of new ideas, that organizations can improve their Innovation Quotient (IQ). Company-wide innovation is not about nurturing solitary genius in sterile laboratories but requires the bubbling enthusiasm of teams, playfully ping-ponging wild ideas, taming them, using old ideas as a foundation for innovation and, finally, carefully hand-holding and nurturing innovative teams through the long and messy process of implementation.

Companies wanting to be innovative need to draw a clear line between thinking and doing. Thinking can be outrageous, intuitive, and dangerous. It can only add new dimensions to understanding the situation. The rules for thinking are different from the rules for doing. Implementation is possible only with a clear foundation of rational thought and practical application. 'Thinking' about building a 2000-crore factory and using the metaphor of a growing tree exercise costs little. Using the laboratory of the mind, we can analyse the different, alternative solutions. Thinking enables us to explore alternatives before choosing the most suitable, profitable and satisfying solution. 'Doing' requires different analytical skills. But many companies make people afraid even to think beyond the beaten path. Today, any company travelling the traditional path may be driven off the road by innovation in technology, as in the case of the textile units in Coimbatore. The rate of change makes it dangerous not to change. The greatest paradox is that the biggest risk of all is not to be innovative, never to do anything new, even at the experimental level. The business or individual who never experiments and continues to do things 'the way we've always done it' feels safe and comfortable, but risks being caught out by changing circumstances. They are liable to wake up one day and find that the established methods are no longer working. 'Bold, speculative, even outrageous thinking, is mainspring innovation. It needs to be converted into product action, in the form of multiple, affordable experiments,' says Vincent Nolan. The key word here is 'affordable' experiments. An experiment should not destroy the company. An experiment should provide feedback and not be judged for its success.

Incubation, Analysis and Implementation

- During idea generation, a list of alternative solutions are generated, seeds are sown.
- During incubation the seeds are allowed to sprout, to grow unobstructed.
- During analysis the plants are pruned and weeds are removed, till only the usable alternatives remain.
- Implementation involves choosing the final solution, planning, developing a detailed roadmap, communicating it to the teams and finally acting on the blueprint.

The MindsPower thinking process maps five key stages:

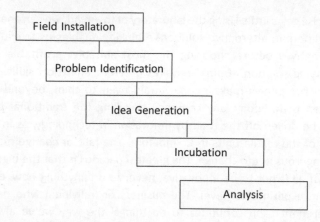

Incubation and Analysis are the key stages in the completion of the Creative Thinking process.

The best ideas are stimulated during incubation

After idea generation, the next step in the thinking process is incubation. After you have spent time collecting the facts and generating ideas, forget the problem. Hand it over to the subconscious to incubate. The subconscious is a vast computer, which stores everything you have ever seen, felt, smelt or experienced. You may read a book, watch a movie, listen to music or ride a bicycle. Incubation after hard work can result in discovery.

Alex Osborne, the advertising genius, said that during incubation, 'I lie like a wet leaf on a log of wood and allow the current to carry me where it will.' Osborne continues, 'When I am thus involved in doing nothing, I receive a constant stream of telegrams from my subconscious.' He feels that he has done his best work when he was really doing nothing.

It was during incubation that Newton discovered the laws of gravity.

Also bear in mind that luck favours the prepared mind. The thought process involved is a cycle, linking preparation, incubation, illumination and verification.

It was while having a bath that Archimedes discovered the laws of displacement.

The Cycle of Incubation

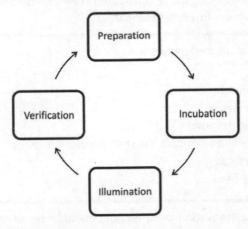

Kekule, after years of tireless effort to understand the benzene molecule, dreamt of a fiery snake chasing its own tail. That led him to the discovery of the benzene ring.

The process of incubation enables you to throw off the shackles of conscious thought and float through the unconscious. The process may last half an hour or a few days. Forget the problem if possible and enjoy a mental holiday.

Tip: The process of incubation can be aided by carrying Post-it notes to record ideas that flash through the mind. Dale Carnegie suggests carrying an envelope into which one can keep dropping slips of paper, as ideas float though one's mind.

Analysis is a corollary to Incubation

In the creative thinking process, Incubation is followed by Analysis. During the process of analysis, apply left-brain thinking—logical, statistical and mathematical. Solutions have to be carefully discussed and the optimum one chosen. The solutions are analysed against the parameters chosen by the problem owner.

Product innovation is not the most important type of innovation, though it is considered the most common type of innovation in Indian companies.

Some prevalent parameters are:

- Time
- Budget
- Convenience
- Human resources
- Goodwill and impact on staff motivation levels
- Aesthetics
- Saving lives

Marketing innovation can affect the brand image of the whole product category. Café Coffee Day and Barista cafés have redefined the coffee break. 'So much can happen over coffee', says one of the advertisements. The success of these cafés has been good for coffee distributors all over India and has given coffee a new brand image.

Political capital

Different parameters find different levels of priority depending on the situation at hand. Let us consider the example of the budget as a parameter and its priority level in different cases. If the problem being discussed was the war in Kargil, political capital and saving lives would be on top of the list. The budget may be irrelevant here. For a company where liquidity is low, cash flow would be the most important concern. For a company facing a crisis, time may be of essence. Big budgets would be tolerated in view of the emergency situation.

While identifying solutions, ensure that there are a wide variety of options to choose from. This makes for a greater possibility that the final option chosen ensures optimal results.

Analysis is the stage just prior to Implementation. Therefore, detailed analysis forms the root to strong implementation.

Time-sharing of holiday cottages created a whole new market for affordable holidays. Today, tractor companies are trying the same concept, where a group of farmers own a tractor together.

Analysis Tip

Go
some
distance
away because
the work appears
smaller and more of it
can be taken in at a glance
and a lack of harmony or proportion is rapidly seen

— Leonardo da Vinci

Implementation: The final stage of the process

The 'reality test' should now be ruthlessly applied. Once implementation starts, every move costs money. This is the last step in the thinking process and all ideas should be carefully studied. Implementing creative ideas and turning them into innovations is a special challenge. It is a process that requires a clear road map and the organizational will to stick to the path. This is where many organizations fail.

An ounce of action is worth tons of e-mail, paper and speeches. Implementation is the key to innovation.

Here is a format for the preparation of a blueprint for the implementation process.

Implementation Map (5W/1H)

	1 month	3 months	6 months	1 year	5 years
WHEN					
WHAT					
WHY					
WHERE					
WHO					
HOW					

The Resource Map (6Ms)

	1 month	3 months	6 months	1 year	5 years
Men					
Material					
Machineries					
Methods					
Markets					
Money					

'Management tends to ignore workers' suggestions about jobs. I have seen engineers ignore comments from workers which would improve the productivity of an individual job. At one point, I noticed hot air holes were crossed, creating a potentially dangerous situation. When I suggested they be altered, the foreman said they had been designed that way by engineers who clearly know better than I, how the plant works. Management obviously is effectively cutting off creativity from a large group of employees who are most likely to make worthwhile suggestions on jobs they are doing. The whole situation carries from a lack of respect for the creativity of the individual. It arises from the view that people ought to be as identical as the cars they make.'

—John F. Awacies

The most essential step is to get total top management support and buy-in for the 5W/1H map. Management would be extremely interested in the result of these actions. The Action Matrix should guide review sessions.

ACTION MATRIX

Measurable Results	1 Month	3 Months	6 Months	1 Year	5 Years
Increasing Profits					
Reducing Costs					
Increasing Customer Satisfaction					
Increasing Employee Commitment					

Wherever innovation is required, the MindsPower process helps you develop a road map.

Star Culture! Managing the process of generating, harvesting and implementing innovations requires long-term commitment. A study of large Indian companies showed that Stars actively fostered a culture of innovation. What is more, they fostered their long-term plans for innovation with adequate resource commitments.

---

*

'Now that you have an idea of the innovation process, let us look at ways to create happy communities, using thinking tools, one at a time,' said Rags.

three

'Who are you, Rags?' I asked incredulously, next day at breakfast.

'A seeker like you,' said he, lightly.

'Are you human or divine?' I asked seriously.

'If you really want to know, everyone is divine. Each of us just has to get rid of all the pollution and smog to manifest the light,' he said, smiling.

'How come you know so much about management?' I asked.

'Life is a classroom. I had a semester on management which, by the way, is really useful in realizing our divine potential.'

'In becoming self-actualized you mean.'

'Whether it is Maslow or the Mahabharata, the purpose of all knowledge is to achieve the highest in ourselves.'

Both of us were silent, reflective, as we went off in the jeep that would take us to the Drukgyal Dzong.

Even in its ruined state, the Dzong retains glimpses of its glory before it was destroyed by fire in 1951. The fire was caused by one of the butter lamps that burned in the Dzong all day!

Both of us stood there in reverence. I thought of all the life-blood of thousands of workmen that had been used in building this edifice. And of the thoughtless way it was destroyed in an instant.

This historical fortress was built in 1647 by Zhaddung Ngwang Namgyal to commemorate his victory over Tibetan invaders. On a ride over bumpy mountain roads, I had become acquainted with muscles and bones which I did not even know existed. I remembered Rima telling me, 'Mae West had curves in places where other people did not even have places.' I grinned to myself. How was she, I wondered? I sent her a hug across the universe on my cellphone.

HOW R U

came an sms the minute my phone could pick up signals.

I messaged back:

GR8. N Bhutan

The signal went off again.

The Dzong was built to protect Bhutan against Tibetan armies. We approached it through a steep cantilevered bridge. The ceilings attract your attention with their beautiful Kalachakra paintings and mandalas. Their view of the cosmos is spellbinding.

'The Taj Mahal was built by 22,000 workers from all over India and it took twenty years to build. Think of the tired, underfed workers building the pyramids, the crack of the whip forcing them to labour far beyond their poor bodies were capable of . . .' said Rags, breaking in exactly where I had left off.

Rags looked wistful as we picked our way through the ruins. I remembered the little girl from Angkor Wat, Cambodia, who slithered out from behind a pillar and in a voice so common to beggars worldwide, wheedled, 'Only one dollar for this purse, only one dollar.' She had brown uncombed locks and honey-brown eyes. She carried an inert little boy on her hip. Suddenly she was joined by a horde of little kids, all tugging at our clothes with sticky fingers and beseeching eyes. We bought a few purses. Everyone wanted to sell us one. A small boy with solemn black eyes stood apart; he asked in beautiful English, 'I am a boy, how about buying it from me?' 'How did you learn to speak like that?' I asked him. 'From tourists,' he said sadly. And I wondered what other unspeakable things they had taught him . . .

When Rags and I reached our hotel, I was exhausted and welcomed a long bath, a cool drink, fresh clothes and total peace; the unrivalled panacea after a long, daunting day.

I went off with Sirius to my room. He was smuggled in under my woolly jacket as the hotel we were staying in did not allow dogs. I did not want to be kept awake all night by his mournful howls from outside.

I sat down and wrote words that rose spontaneously from the depths of my mind:

The sands of eternity

The desert storms
Have scattered wide
The sinuous strength
The Sculptor's arm

The flashing brilliance of his glance
But his thoughts
Fragile as butterfly wings
Remain
On Immutable stone
Unchanged
Through dark centuries
Unmoved
By the endless caravans of those who loved
By the ceaseless tears of those who lost
By the winner's lust for blood and gain
By the loser's hopeless cry of pain
By the tinkling laughter of dancing girls
By the artless charm of a baby's curls.
The potter mingles with the dust
From which the pot is made.
It survives him
Who can make it,
And break it.

The next day we pulled on our walking shoes for a long trek, a long walk, all uphill through fragrant, thick pine forests high up in the mountains. The air was redolent with the tangy smell of cypress, which is the national tree of Bhutan; its dried needles are used in worship here. We spied the Taktsang monastery clinging precariously to the forbidding granite cliff that rises 250 metres above the valley. It is also called the Tiger's Nest and is beautifully painted with fragile pagodas, spires, roofs, mud and stone in natural pigments and earth colours. The walk takes three hours. The building was built without a blueprint, and without nails, following the pattern straight from the builder's mind. How did they manage to carry materials and men to this precarious spot, I wondered.

Guru Padmasambhava is believed to have flown into that spot on the back of a flying tigress in the seventh century. He is said to have meditated for three years, three months and three days and is believed to have subdued the evil demons that resisted the spread of Buddhism in the Paro valley. The monastery built to mark the spot remains a place of pilgrimage for every Bhutanese at least once in their lives. Rags explained that most of the material used was local.

'What do you feel about retreating to a monastery?' I asked Rags, who had spread a blanket and was basking in the cool, caressing winter sun.

'No rest for the wicked,' he said to me. 'You have a lot to do. Your karma is to serve others and improve the Happiness Quotient of others.'

'Why can't I be like you?' I asked mutinously.

'Focus on your duty. My path and karma are different.' He turned on his side and fell asleep. I kicked a stone resentfully down the slope.

Then I reached for a cigarette. 'Do you want to taste like an ashtray to your beloved?' asked Rags lazily.

'Wow! That's a great slogan.'

'Oh, it's from one of the most effective anti-smoking campaigns ever.' Definitely better than campaigns that threaten you with lung cancer! I floated off into a vague daydream about kisses . . .

How to work up the courage to ask for some? From someone who looked like she might slap me if I got out of line?

I looked at the black cloth folder Rags had handed me before copping out of the conversation.

* *

41

Knowledge@Wharton

Nightly Business Report

PBS Business Program concept

The top 30 innovations in the last 30 years chosen out of 1200 suggestions by a panel of 8 judges.

The list is as follows, in order of importance:

1. Internet, broadband, World Wide Web (browser and html)
2. PC/laptop computers
3. Mobile phones
4. E-mail
5. DNA testing and sequencing/Human genome mapping
6. Magnetic Resonance Imaging (MRI)
7. Microprocessors
8. Fiber optics
9. Office software (spreadsheets, word processors)
10. Non-invasive laser/robotic surgery (laparoscopy)
11. Open source software and services (e.g. Linux, Wikipedia)
12. Light emitting diodes (LED)
13. Liquid crystal display (LCD)
14. Global Positioning Systems (GPS)
15. Online shopping/ecommerce/auctions (e.g. eBay)
16. Media file compression (jpeg, mpeg, mp3)
17. Microfinance
18. Photovoltaic Solar Energy
19. Large-scale wind turbines
20. Social networking via the Internet
21. Graphic user interface(GUI)
22. Digital photography/videography
23. Radio Frequency Identification (RFID) and applications (e.g. EZ Pass)
24. Genetically modified plants
25. Bio fuels
26. Barcodes and scanners

27. Automated Teller Machines (ATM)
28. Stents
29. SRAM flash memory
30. Anti-retroviral treatment for AIDS

**

'Not even one from India,' I said, surprised.

'Big, game-changing innovations are not everything. Every day, Indian mothers are innovating: bringing up children, feeding, clothing and educating them and endowing them with knowledge of self, ideals of truth and duty, arming them with the pride of nationhood, on less than two dollars a day. That requires minute-to-minute innovation. It is a true miracle greater than any at Lourdes!' said Rags feelingly.

'I thought everything that can be invented has been invented. At least that is what Charles H. Duell, director of the US patent office, said in 1899,' I recalled.

'All of us know the story of Alfred Nobel who saw his epitaph when he was still alive as "the man who discovered gunpowder". He instituted the Nobel Prize to wipe out his reputation as the merchant of death,' Rags reminded me. 'Do you remember that unforgettable picture of a small girl, Phuc, running naked down a road in Vietnam? Water boils at 100 degrees celsius. Napalm generates temperatures of 800 to 1200 degrees celsius. Phuc had half her body cooked by third degree burns and was not expected to live. She lived after a fourteen-month hospital stay and seventeen operations. The photographer, Nick, helped her. Today she is an effective and outspoken peace activist. She really knows about the tragedy of war in her own body and soul. Anyway, Dr Louis Fieser, the Harvard professor who discovered napalm to kill the pernicious crab grass,

43

burning its seeds and leaving good grass unharmed, says that he is not responsible for the use it was put to in America's war in Vietnam . . .'

Interesting! But this did not give me any ideas on how to proceed with Rima. I wanted to say I loved her in all the languages known to man. Maybe I could start with my own mother tongue Tulu.

'The human mind has the capacity to store 7550 volumes of encyclopedia, according to Carl Sagan,' I said to fill the gap.

'No wonder you were a quizzing wizard in college,' quipped Rags. 'So why are you filling yours with trivia?' he asked.

'Touché,' I said and went off to play with Sirius.

'Happy morning,' said Rags when he woke me as the first light of dawn filtered in.

'Time to get the blood circulating,' he decreed, and put me through a bout of spot jogging. 'Your blood will be shaken like medicine in a bottle,' he said, 'no sediments.'

Over a breakfast of fresh fruit, toast and butter tea (*suja*), we talked. He told me how in 1974 Jigme Singye Wangchuk, the king of Bhutan, returned to his country after a liberal education in India and UK and came up with the idea of measuring a country's progress through its Gross National Happiness—something that went far beyond GDP.

Gross National Happiness (GNH) includes four pillars:

1. Encouraging sustainable use of the environment
2. Preserving and promoting cultural heritage
3. Establishing good governance
4. Economic growth and development

Today GNH is being slowly converted into a workable set of standard indicators.

The new GNH measures nine different domains:

1. Health
2. Education
3. Living standards
4. Time use
5. Environment quality
6. Culture
7. Community vitality
8. Governance
9. Psychological well-being

It is being used in Thailand, tried out in Canada, and being considered for use in the UK and Australia. The UN is now asking member nations to come up with their own idea of Gross National Happiness.

'How to sell this idea to political leaders?' asked Rags ruminatively.

I stared at him resentfully. 'Don't tell me you want me to do this too?'

'You will have a networked team worldwide,' he said, eyes twinkling, 'and the World Wide Web. You just need to go viral . . .'

Was this the uncertain path less travelled?

'First protect Mother Earth,' Rags said. 'Bhutan has developed high environmental protection standards—the use of plastic bags is banned here.'

'Maybe they are too poor to afford it,' I said flippantly.

'They have managed to create a peaceful and harmonious society that actively protects its rich culture and profound Buddhist traditions.'

'They can't afford anything else. There is nothing much anyone can do here except be quiet,' was my chirpy retort.

'Why are you so negative? They have three major economic opportunities: agriculture, tourism and hydro-electric power. The three major rivers of the subcontinent—the Ganges, the Indus and the Brahmaputra—have their source in the Himalayas. The rivers of Bhutan are part of the Brahmaputra system. Do you know that Bhutan provides the medicinal herbs for many ingredients of Tibetan and Chinese medicine? The holistic Sowa Rigpa system uses over 400 medicinal plants grown in the region. Most of them grow in altitudes of above 4000 metres. The medicines are supported by spiritual counselling. Hot mineral baths at the Gasa spring or hot stone baths in Thimpu add to the "feel good" factor.'

Rags told me that like Ayurveda and Siddha, the Sowa Rigpa traditional system of medicine synthesized the knowledge of many cultures.

'Listening and accepting the best of other systems is critical to innovation, isn't it?' I offered.

'Listening for value, assuming that even an enemy, a child or a puppy can tell you something, is key. The Bhutanese have seamlessly borrowed ideas from the Indian science of health and the Chinese system of reading the twelve pulses. They also add to the mix, bad karma and evil spirits. The patient receives physical, mental and spiritual help to heal himself,' said Rags.

'The art of medicine consists of amusing the patient, while Nature cures the disease,' I said, quoting Voltaire. 'Look at the grinding poverty around you,' I challenged him.

Rags said, 'How can they maintain environmental sustainability and happiness and be economically successful?'

'How do you say they are happy when life expectancy is 66 years and they have a 7.2 per million infant mortality rate?' I questioned.

I showed him a poem written by my mom for her great-great-grandmother who, like 250,000 women every year even in 2011, died in childbirth.

Ode to my great-grandmother

Muthu
Born: 1874   Died: 1891

Fragile, fair and seventeen
She was a pearl that bled to death
On a snowy couch
Fed from silver plates,
She bled to death.
At the moment of giving life,
She bled to death
In silken garments
In a pillared hall,
Amidst the shrieking of a newborn baby's call
She breathed her last.
Life ebbed out of her
As it surged, through
An orphaned baby's heart.

'Do you know health care and education are free till Class 10 in Bhutan?' Rags asked. 'Bhutan has become a parliamentary democracy in March 2008. But they have the most beautiful fairytale king and queen and a castle: Punaka Dzong—the palace of great happiness—where the young king and queen got married recently. And do you know they are the first country in the world to ban the sale of tobacco?'

'Really!' I said disbelievingly.

'You don't have to be sarcastic. They are at least trying . . .' he said reproachfully.

'How come they are not going all out to promote tourism? It's so difficult to get here . . .'

'This policy is influenced by the concept of Gross National Happiness. The country intentionally develops slowly and learns from mistakes made by other countries. They believe in the high benefit, low impact philosophy.'

Ma was right, I thought, when she said 'Haste makes waste'. Like she wrote once, 'You cannot command the flower to bloom at your will, or the tree to grow by your daily planner, or force a child to open his mind.'

Maybe companies and families use too much force to speed up the process of unfolding and evolution. How often I've been shouted at—'Hurry up, don't dawdle!'

I turned to a page of my mom's last book of poems (unpublished).

Time, the cruel one

For an endless hour
My son drinks his orange juice
I, harassed, rushing off to work,
Spank him with a ruthless hand,
And stand over him, while he drinks between stifled sobs.
Today with nothing to do, I watch . . .
He holds it to the light
And sees the dance of sunbeams,
Through his jewelled orange drink
He dribbles it down his chin in an orgy of joy

And blows incandescent bubbles
He dips his fingers into its coolness
He pours a little on the ground and follows the meandering stream
With his head against the floor.
A winding miniature river
Wandering out to the door. . .
I wish I did not have to rush, ever.

My cellphone flashed a message:

> **MISS U**

But the signal was gone again before I could message Rima back with a fervent 'Me too'.

'The New GNH can help shape an economic infrastructure capable of promoting a future world where the environment and culture are protected,' said Rags, reading from a newspaper.

I was deep in thought about things I had never thought about. I had spent years cocooned in the concerns of just my immediate family and office team. Rags had opened the floodgates . . .

And it was an overwhelming experience.

Before I slept I wrote a poem for Rima, which the universe had just whispered in my ear.

Alchemy

You've opened the doors
Long shut tight
And set free
The imprisoned laughter
Of a child long dead

Thrown open the rusted shutters
And let in the whirlwind
Of a million unexplored dreams.
Awakened a storm of thoughts
That take flight to unknown lands
You've made me reach out
Beyond the far reaches of myself
To explore limitless inner worlds.
And touched with magic the trifles of everyday
Like the touch of the moon
On the silent ocean
Transforming it into a metalled silver pathway
To the stars.

I would post it to her the old, forgotten way, I resolved,
using the most beautiful stamps in the world, from Bhutan.

four

Rags and I discussed what a sustainable environment means.

Environmental quality is a general term which can refer to varied characteristics that relate to the natural environment as well as the built-up environment, such as air and water purity, or pollution, buildings and infrastructure, noise and the potential effects which such characteristics may have on physical and mental health caused by human activities.

'Treat the earth like a friend. Replace whatever you take from her, with love,' said Rags.

The air was pure and fresh. The silence enveloped us as we walked through the cool valley. I remembered my grandfather reading from the Atharva Veda:

Peace be to earth and to airy spaces.
Peace be to heaven, peace to the waters,
Peace to the plants and peace to the trees
May all the Gods grant me peace.

—Atharva Veda 19.9.14

Coloured prayer flags fluttered everywhere in the cool mountain breeze. 'Prayer flags are put up for good luck. They are also supposed to help dead souls find their new lives. The more festoons of such flags, the better for the souls in limbo. The flags represent the pancha bhutas or elements in five colours: yellow, green, red, white and blue; 108 flags are used when someone dies,' said Rags.

'But thousands of young trees are cut every year to make prayer flags,' he continued. 'The citizens have not been persuaded to use steel instead of wood and now the government is trying to convert them to bamboo. It is estimated that 60,000 trees were felled for flagposts in 2007–08.'

'Why not re-use old flag posts?' I asked.

'It would show a lack of true caring and effort and reduce the merit earned,' said Rags. 'As a result of the hydro-electric projects and flags, the threat to the forest is increasing.'

'We need to stop doing many things to achieve a sustainable, clean environment,' I said.

'Look!' he said, pointing at the limpid lake. 'No plastic bags, no empty shampoo sachets.'

Talking of shampoo sachets, he spoke of how a young doctor in Tamil Nadu had the idea of putting a rupee's worth of shampoo into a sachet. Thanks to that idea, today every village girl has access to shampoo!

'The principle of small, affordable quantity, while maintaining quality, is something that will enable us to take the world's goodies to the bottom of the pyramid,' Rags said. 'But perhaps we should consider how to make the sachets biodegradable. Perhaps we could put the shampoo into pharmaceutical capsules like those that are used for eye drops. See what the Tatas have done with the Nano— the Rs 1 lakh car. Today all of Europe wants the car. This is innovation blowback for you. Rich countries want what poor countries are creating because it is better for planet Earth; it reduces one's carbon footprint.'

'I have a friend who has decided to buy the Nano in seven colours: one for each day of the week,' I said. 'White for Monday, red for Tuesday, green for Wednesday, yellow for Thursday, blue for Friday, silver for Saturday and black for Sunday—to attract good planetary energy. He is a dashing young millionaire, Rs 7 lakh is nothing to him! And by the way, why can't we all wash our hair with amla and shikakai? I bet I'd have more hair if I did that!' Rags laughed appreciatively and I saw Rima's lovely hair fly in a cloud before me. Good God! What was happening to me? I seemed to remember her more in her absence than in her presence.

'This place reminds me of a trip I made to Valli Malai near Vellore,' said Rags. 'Lord Muruga fell in love with Valli on this lovely hill. One can see manjal (turmeric) stains where Valli the gypsy bathed in shallow rainwater puddles, watched by resplendent peacocks.'

'Nature is beautiful,' I said. '"Go back to grandmother's remedy" is a good way of innovating. The Managing Director of Finolex Cables had a problem with rats biting his cables. He tried everything, used lots of chemicals. Nothing worked till he saw his mother using neem oil on her grandson's thumb to prevent him from sucking it. The rats didn't like the neem oil either. I bet neem oil is a lot less toxic than many pesticides and equally effective.'

Rags was thrilled with what I was saying. 'You are a really innovative cat!' he said. I put up my collar and took a mock bow.

'Why can't we preserve our spaces like this in India?' I asked.

I saw Rima smiling at me in my mind's eye.

'Absence is like a wind to the fire of love. Minor infatuations get blown out. The love of your life gets blown up into a mighty fire,' said Rags, grinning at me.

'Don't talk rubbish,' I said curtly.

But as we walked on in silence, my thoughts became clearer to me. I realized that Rima was the kind of girl I would have taken home to my mom, if only she had been there ...

During her last battle against cancer my mother had written a bunch of letters to her future daughter-in-law and left it with her few jewels in the locker. 'To be given to the love of your life, my daughter in love, Junie', she had written on the sealed cover. Was Rima the one?

I remembered Mom's long battle against cancer. 'When doctors say that the side effects of chemotherapy are tolerable or acceptable, they are talking about life-threatening things,' Rose Kushner, a cancer survivor, wrote. 'But if you just vomit so hard that you break the blood vessels in your eyes ... they don't consider that even mentionable. And they certainly don't care if you're bald,' she wrote sarcastically. 'The smiling oncologist does not know whether his patients vomit or not.' I remembered how bravely my mother faced the toxic cancer treatment. I was looking for someone like her, loving, beautiful and brave. I pulled out her book of handwritten poems and read:

Pain

Pain washes over me
Like the battalions of rain
On the windshield
Of an abandoned car.

She told me once that every soul passes through many lifetimes, discarding bodies like worn out clothes. 'If one were to pool the milk of mothers who have fed us in our many lifetimes, we would drown in it,' she concluded, quoting from the sayings of the Buddha. My memories of Mom were sad and beautiful. I could still hear her voice in my ear. And I felt she was still with me, a part of my being.

Rags opened a sleek black folder entitled 'Emotional Health Assessment'.

'Do you get angry often?' he asked.

I remembered the pounding rage in my head every time my boss played politics with me.

'Anger is one of the most destructive emotions,' said Rags. 'When you get angry, thirty-six different chemicals pour into the blood. Chemicals like adrenaline, histamine, blood glucose. The heart rate goes up, the pulse rate goes up. All parts of the brain are switched off, except what you need to kill or run.'

Devastating stuff, which was the state of my bloodstream routinely when I was at work. I was aghast. Rags looked at me affectionately and said, 'Try to foster positive emotions like love, compassion, laughter, courage and wonder: these five emotions from the Nava Rasa fill your body with the chemicals of healing and happiness: endorphins and serotonins.'

I sat quietly, leaning against the soft, grassy slope. 'Let thoughts flow like a movie in the head—just watch them,' said Rags. He handed me the black folder.

**

Your Emotional Health Assessment

Answer Yes (Y) / No (N)   Y   N

1. Do you keep in touch with world events?
2. Are you up-to-date in your chosen subject?
3. Do you have clear, written goals?
4. Are your actions geared towards those goals?
5. Do you deal with anger in a healthy way?
6. Can you disagree without losing control?
7. Do you have a few close friends who care for you?
8. Are you friendly with your neighbours?
9. Do you pray or meditate every day?
10. Are you worried about tasks and deadlines?
11. Do you proactively seek new opportunities and expect to be successful?
12. Are you collaborative?
13. Do you fear not living up to expectations?
14. Do you compare yourself with others and feel jealous?
15. Do you worry about how your bosses regard you?
16. Do work situations make you angry often?
17. Are you afraid of losing your job or being overlooked for a promotion?
18. Do you continue to work even if you are exhausted?
19. Do you stay at your workplace for more than ten hours?
20. Do you routinely eat your meals late?

Score
Good: 9 or more Ns
Adequate: 6 or more Ns
Poor: Less than 6 Ns

**

We went through the questionnaire together. Some of the questions were about worry. I did tend to worry a lot, I realized, mostly about things that never happened. 'Worry just eats away at your happiness like mice in a godown,' said Rags, reminding me that 30 per cent of India's food grains are eaten up by rodents. The Chinese apparently found a solution for this. They declared that they would pay for every rat tail that was delivered to the authorities. The rat menace just disappeared overnight!

'How can we save Mother Nature?' I asked.

Rags was silent for a while. 'How do you think leather towns like Vaniyambadi can do it? Or a tee-shirt paradise like Tirupur, how could they be the world's top producers of tee-shirts and not pollute the earth?' he said.

I remembered how I had seen the dark-green colour of water within a tender coconut in that town. Coloured by the dyes poured into the earth. If the dyes could permeate the inside of the coconut, I could imagine the effect it would have on a baby inside the womb. I remembered Minamata, Japan.

Rags and I spoke about it. He recalled the unforgettable picture of a worn-out mother bathing the ruined body of her forty-year-old son. 'The company paid through its nose to those families for pouring toxic mercury waste into the river. But can money really compensate a mother who has to watch her forty-year-old son crawling like a baby and change his diapers?'

'How can anyone put profits above the rights of a person to live a simple human life?' I asked. Sirius was walking beside me, his furry tail held aloft like a flag. His ears alertly lifted to catch the slightest alien sound.

'I don't think you have been reading the newspapers,' said Rags, referring to the mining scandals. 'Everything is for sale. Mother Earth has been defiled and no one cares.'

'What about the women who hugged the trees in the Chipko movement so that they could not be cut? What about the one lakh trees my company is planting as part of our corporate social responsibility?'

'Mere drops in the ocean.'

'I like what Siruthuli, the social activist group, has done for the river Noyyal,' I said, handing over a paper cutting.

Drop by drop

I think of the river Noyyal as a living goddess, blessing everything she touches with the green of life.

As a young woman, I was fully absorbed in the task of working with my husband's successful auto parts business and a growing family. I was proud of living in Coimbatore, called the Manchester of South India. Until I saw what we had done to the beautiful river Noyyal. The price of industrial growth was steep. The limpid river had become nothing but a rotten sewer. UNDP had just declared that Coimbatore had recorded the fastest depletion of ground water levels in the whole world! According to law, borewells could not be drilled. But there were 400,000 borewells dug into the dying heart of Mother Earth. In 2003 there was an acute water shortage.

It was great to be part of a group of industrialists waiting to solve this problem. The problem was a many-headed hydra. Multifactorial in nature, it needed the whole city to unite to solve it. So we started . . . drop by drop. Today, NABARD has adopted 1300 hectares as a watershed which will rejuvenate 500 sq. kms of the river.

We tried to involve the whole city in a project named 'Noyyalukku Nooru'. By paying a hundred rupees for the Noyyal, citizens could contribute their mite to the river of funds. 15,000 students participated in a rally. World Water Day on 22 March is celebrated. All citizens were encouraged to open a Water Savings Account. Eco Forums were started in 32 colleges. The classic dance drama *Silappadigaram* re-created the heritage of the river Noyyal. Noyyal yathra took over 1 lakh citizens on a pilgrimage to the pristine origin of the river Noyyal. Nadi karai nagarceyakam involved over 8,000 students in learning about river valley civilizations. Over 3,000 farmers were involved in zero budget farming, promoting organic and natural farming. Love of the mother river was promoted and a programme initiated to fight the monster of pollution: over 10,000 people participated. Finally, the technical advisory committee is working on clearing up the river. I am proud to be part of an intensive endeavour in water resources management, afforestation, waste management and water awareness programmes.

It has been an eventful journey which has enlivened my life with the pure beauty which only water can endow.

Mrs Vanitha Mohan
SIRUTHULI

We talked about the healing of 500 square kilometres of a river by involving all those who lived on the banks of the river in Coimbatore. 'The river is now worshipped as a goddess—Pachai Nayaki,' I said. 'Children write about her sacred waters. Why can't we persuade more cities to do it? Why can't we?'

Rags put out an implacable hand and asked, 'What have *you* done?' He recited from memory, from the musical *Look Beyond Yourself*.

(Busy road. People walking like robots.)

Chorus: Have you seen your neighbour lately?
Have you seen your neighbour lately,
Have you seen his eyes, his face, his life?

Have you ever looked
At the milk abandoned at his door
At the child resigned to its fate
Have you seen the plants drooping
Right outside his door?

As you walk through the faceless crowds
Have you seen him crying aloud?

(We cut to a mother whose child has died—a boy murdered
for his watch.)

Mother: He was so young, so beautiful. How could you
watch him die on the street?

How could you watch him bleed? How could you
shut your ears to his cries?

Chorus: What would you do
Would you rush to his aid
Or would you cower by the gate
Would you refuse to see
What is happening outside your door?

Where were you when the children cried?
Where were you when the homes were burnt?
Where were you when the trees were cut?
Where were you when the deer were shot
Through the heart?

Did you act?
Did you write?
Did you speak?
Did you walk out?
Did you cry out?
Or did you watch in silence?
As the world died.

'Each of us have a personal responsibility to fulfil,' said Rags. 'Each of us has a personal duty to do something to spread the message. Use the Internet for life-changing, life-affirming activities, stop complaining. Do . . . do something!'

'Do you know the cost of crime in society?' he continued. 'The cost is measured on the amounts we spend on courts and prisons, burglar alarms, security guards, hospital costs due to assault victim treatments. The amount saved by a lower crime rate can be used for development.'

'Sometimes the decision between livelihood, education and environment are not so easy,' I pointed out. 'The Kolleru lake, at one end of West Godavari District in Andhra, is home to many birds, including grey pelicans. Those living in the Komatilanka village are literally cut off from the outside world. Country boats are the only way out. Schoolchildren suffer the most. Two positions for teachers are vacant for years. Hardly two students from the local primary school decide to seek higher education. A road will disturb wild life and affect the aqua culture, but without a road, education is compromised. How to balance these two important requirements?'

'So think it through, involve all stakeholders. Don't be an armchair environmentalist,' said Rags.

We walked home, tired and worn out, full of deep thoughts. A green folder was waiting for me on my pillow.

Sirius hates it when I read. Or do anything that does not involve him. But I had little choice.

**

Sustainable Development

The carbon footprint is measured by the CO_2 or other greenhouse gases created by an object or action. We need to aim at a lower carbon footprint. Ten tonnes per year is what Americans want to achieve. Climate change is a big deal and it's manmade. It's not just CO_2, there is methane (CH_2), released from mining, agriculture and landfill sites. It is twenty-five times more potent then CO_2. Then there is Nitrous Oxide (N_2O) which is 300 times more potent, released due to certain industrial activities; CFCs released by refrigerators are several thousand times more potent.

Driving a car impacts the environment. It is not only emissions that come out of the exhaust pipe, but all emissions that take place when oil is extracted, shipped, refined into fuel and transported to the petrol station. What about the industrial emissions caused by producing and maintaining the car? Planes in the sky have even greater impact, maybe four times that of similar emissions at ground level.

Mad cow disease is caused by feeding cows and chicken non-vegetarian food—when offal is added to animal feeds.

Look at the impact of e-mail: McAfee estimates that 78 per cent of all incoming e-mails are spam. 62 trillion spam messages are sent every year.

**

'The turning point is here. If we do not read the warnings, revolution is at our door. Let us not be caught unawares like the French queen, Marie Antionette, who on learning that there was no bread advised starving peasants to eat cake!' said Rags. 'We can still save planet Earth by being proactive. Start by carrying a reusable shopping bag. At least don't encourage plastic use yourself.'

How was it possible for India to halt its development to be like Bhutan, I wondered. How could development be balanced against a pristine environment? In Bhutan no one blows horns and there are no traffic lights. There is no loud, intrusive filmi music anywhere—just silence and the murmur of Nature.

Before I fell asleep I wrote a poem for Rima. I had still not posted the last one . . .

Awakening

You awaken the clamour
Of a thousand violins in my blood
You have invaded my dreams
And crept into
The last hidden crevice of my soul
So that every cell in my unwilling body
Calls your name.

five

Next morning, I found Rags standing on his head.

'Today, let us turn everything upside down,' he said as he sprang to his feet. 'Why can't each one of us take responsibility for keeping the earth green and beautiful instead of depending on the government to do so? Just like each of us keeps the toilets inside our house clean, why can't we keep our streets, forests and rivers clean?'

Rags took me through a case study on toilets. Sulabh (as in 'easy') is the name of the company providing public toilets nationwide. At the Sulabh International Museum of Toilets, which has been visited by 2.2 million people, and where gold-plated loos take your breath away, you are stunned to realize that 2.5 billion people have no toilets at home. They use the streets, fields, corners of homes instead.

Bindeshwar Pathak, the founder of Sulabh, is a Brahmin who once had to swallow *panchagavya*, a mixture of cow dung, urine and other similar ingredients, as an antidote to a scavenger's touch. It was put together by his grandmother for him after he was touched by a cleaner of toilets.

In 1977, Bindeshwar came up with an idea for a decentralized waste water treatment plant which recycles water, produces bio-gas for cooking and produces odourless bio-fertilizer. He got the idea from an adivasi from Madhya Pradesh in a village near Indore. The methane gas produced could be used for cooking. This idea has now spread to schools in Africa.

Lesson Learnt: To innovate, become innocent. Talk to your grandmother, walk to the slum and observe the child, listen to the tribal. Look for the impact of your innovation on his face.

Bindeshwar Pathak created a twin pit, pour-flush, comfort toilet. Using just a mug of water, it needs no sewage system. The waste in the pit becomes valuable fertilizer. Today he has built 7500 'Use and Pay' Sulabh Shauchalayas and pit latrines in 1.2 million homes. Users pay and use the toilets, liberating thousands of scavengers from the soul-sapping task of manually carrying away night soil. Sulabh has annual revenues of Rs125 crore.

The Paro to Thimpu trek starts above Ta Dzong and ends with the descent into Thimpu. It takes four to six days, and the maximum altitude is over 4000 metres. We trekked through green valleys, several high altitude lakes and some mountain passes. One of the bubbling rivers, Pa-chu, Wang-chu or Thim-chu, kept us company. The Manas river is the largest river system of Bhutan, among its four major river systems; the other three are Amo-chu or Torsa, Wang-chu or Raidak, and Mo-chu or Sankosh. The Manas river with its deceptive calm has strong undercurrents, just like the mind. We unexpectedly came upon the national flower of Bhutan, a rare blue poppy. It is a plant that lives several years and blooms only once during its long life.

We were helped in pitching our tent by a team which dealt with the ponies, the tents and cooking. They were silent and efficient and left the campsites pristine.

We walked through lush meadows of artlessly blossoming wildflowers and became attentive to bird song. We also discussed many things about innovation. The feeling of physical and mental well-being is a calm, secret wellspring of joy. 'Get rid of negative thoughts. If a viper lives in your room and you wish to sleep peacefully, you must first chase it out, says the Buddha. Fill your mind with beautiful thoughts,' Rags said.

He gave me a dried peepal leaf, edged in gold paint. The words of Buddha were etched on it:

With loving kindness and compassion train your mind to be broad as the earth and unlimited as the sky, deep as a big river and soft as well-tanned leather. Your suffering is my suffering, your happiness is my happiness. Just as a mother realizes her motherhood by loving her child, then the child reacting to that love feels safe and at ease. Like rain falling equally on all, a father in his compassion and a mother in her loving kindness, smoothes the friction of birth and death.

'I really love what the Buddha says,' I said dreamily.

'Every religion has the same wonderful ideas,' said Rags.

It was dusk when we descended into Thimpu. There were no bright street lights, not even in the lower market which sold provisions and inexpensive garments on the pavement. It was cold, about 12 degrees, with a chill wind. Many closed shop before 5 p.m. and everyone went home to curl up with a snack of crisp fried raw rice and a cup of the homemade wine, ara. We took a winding mountain road that took us above the city, giving us a magnificent view of the Trashichhoe Dzong, otherwise called the Fortress of the Auspicious Religion. This fairytale castle is now used for government offices and of course as a dwelling for 200 monks: the religious and secular are often found together in Bhutan.

Built in 1216 and superbly proportioned, the Trashichhoe Dzong was badly damaged during a battle with the Drukpas in the middle ages. In 1641 Ngawang Namgyal rebuilt the dzong. Following a fire in 1772, it was rebuilt again at the bottom of the valley where it now stands. Unlike other dzongs, this one has three entrances: one for citizens, leading to the administrative establishment; another to the monastic section in whose courtyard the tsechu is performed annually; and the third only for royalty.

Unless you have official business, you can only enter the monastic section to visit the main Lhakhang through the vast courtyard.

This new Lhakhang Sarp (built in 1907) is in the centre of the courtyard. We were allowed to enter this temple and visited the top floor with its outstanding mandalas and a striking statue of Guru Padmasambhava. There was a magnificent 'Wheel of Life' painted on the exterior of the building where the monks assembled. We left by the well-crafted wooden bridge that spans the river at the base of the dzong.

On the outskirts of Thimpu, the air is fragrant with fallen needles of the pine-like cypress, the national tree of Bhutan. It has a sharp distinctive fragrance, like eucalyptus. The leadership of Bhutan has certainly moved slowly towards development. The Paro airport was built only in 1983. All developmental plans give due importance to the environment.

- 80 per cent of the land has forest cover.
- Small dams are built to generate hydroelectric power.
- Mining and quarrying are controlled.
- Felling of trees is restricted.
- Tourism is controlled.
- Weaving is encouraged (in the past, taxes could be paid by cloth).

This is a land of incredible diversity in plant life. 70 per cent of the land is covered by forests, with an incredible diversity of 5000 species of plants, 600 types of orchids and forty-five varieties of rhododendrons and 400 types of mushrooms.

Rags told me that the rhododendrons bloomed all over the hills between March and May and the whole hillside was ablaze then with brilliant red flowers. White magnolias and dapne scented the still air. At our feet was a magic carpet of tiny flowers and gracefully waving grass.

'What do you do for exercise?' asked Rags as we climbed the steep hill.

'I hit the gym on Sundays,' I said, guiltily remembering all the weekends I had slept in after those drunken binges.

'You need to use it, or you'll lose it. Don't think you can start when you are fat and forty. It will be too late then.' I noticed him looking at the slight paunch that was hidden under my loose tee-shirt.

'Just make sure you use each and every muscle regularly,' he said. Ever since we had come to Bhutan, we always seemed to be walking or moving. I hadn't needed either alcohol or tranquilizers to fall into a deep, dreamless sleep.

We walked through pristine green landscapes and stopped by the river. We decided to stop over and our helpers pitched the tent on the riverside. The air was clean and fresh. I felt lightheaded. 'Part of it is the altitude,' said Rags.

We ate hot, freshly cooked food. The authentic Bhutanese food was fresh and appetizing. Crisp, lightly cooked broccoli with diced carrots and green beans, bursting with colour and antioxidants. Red hand-pounded rice with potato wedges. Sliced mushrooms tossed in melted cheese. 'Food tastes so good if we don't cook it to death,' said Rags. 'Or smother it with spices,' said I, enjoying the subtle flavours of lemon grass, pepper and slit green chillies, which allowed each vegetable flavour to come through. Hot butter tea (suja) completed the meal.

Rags then proceeded to teach me how to breathe so that every part of my body felt full of life. 'Breathing correctly is the most important thing you can do,' he said. 'Spine erect,' he reminded me. 'Sit comfortably, let your flesh hang on your shoulders like a coat on a hanger. When you are depressed, you slump. This further cuts down your intake of oxygen. And you feel even worse as carbon dioxide accumulates.'

We woke to the song of birds and washed in the clean stream wending its way through our impromptu campsite. Suddenly I wished Rima was with us. She would have loved this journey. We were such good friends. Maybe trying to make it anything else would turn a first-rate friendship into a third-rate love affair.

Rags was looking at me searchingly. 'So who is she?' he asked.

'Who?' I said.

'Whoever is making you look so goofy.'

I ignored him and started petting Sirius, our curly haired friend. I realized that Rima was the cause of a smile that could not be wiped off my face. Whenever I thought of her, my face broke into a goofy grin.

'We can transform ourselves and others,' Rags said. 'Norman Cousins recovered from what is usually a fatal disease through laughter, love and music. You can be happy by taking regular laughter breaks. There are a number of causes for high blood pressure and heart disease like heredity, obesity, smoking and excessive intake of saturated fats. But stress is one of the main factors. Laughter definitely helps control blood pressure by reducing the release of stress-related hormones and bringing relaxation.'

He told me that in experiments it has been proved that there is a drop of 10–20 mm in blood pressure after participating for ten minutes in a laughter session. It does not mean that those who are taking 2–3 tablets for high blood pressure every day will be completely cured. Maybe, you will require two tablets if you are taking three, or if you are a borderline high blood pressure patient, you may not require any medication after some time. It takes years to develop high blood pressure. It cannot be reversed in a few days or a month. But laughter will definitely exercise some control and arrest further progress of the disease.

If you are at high risk of developing heart disease, laughter could be the best preventive medicine. Those who are suffering from heart disease and have stabilized on medication will find that laughter improves the blood circulation and oxygen supply to the heart muscles. Due to improvement of blood circulation there are less chances of forming a clot. Those who have had heart attacks or have undergone bypass surgery can also participate in laughter therapy.

Rima's infectious laughter rang in my ears.

We had known each other for two years. But we still were 'just friends', as the gossip magazines say. Was I commitment phobic like so many of my generation?

Rags handed over a questionnaire.

**

Physical Wellness

Your Physical Health Assessment
Answer Yes (Y) / No (N)   Y   N

1. Do you have a family doctor?
1. Have you had your annual health check-up?
2. Do you respond to the doctor's advice and your body's signals?
3. Are you free of daily medicines?
4. Is the air you breathe clean?
5. Have you learned pranayama and yoga exercises and practise them regularly?
6. Do you pay enough attention to exercise and diet?
7. Do you set apart time for exercise on a regular basis?
8. Do you eat high-quality food chosen to give you energy?
9. Do you have access to clean water?
10. Are you free of tobacco, drugs or alcohol? (Write no if even one is present in your life)
11. Are you able to avoid negative emotions?
12. Do you sleep for eight hours at night?
13. Do you take care of minor health disturbances and pains?
14. Do you live in a clean, garbage-free area?

15. Do you live among people who are positive and peaceful?
16. Do you watch television for less than an hour a day?
17. Do you walk short distances and avoid vehicles?
18. Do you drink less than three cups of coffee a day?
19. Are you aware of any chronic illnesses in your family: diabetes, heart trouble, high BP, or ulcers?
20. Are all children in your family alive and healthy?

Score
Good: 12 or more Ys
Adequate: 6 or more Ys
Poor: Less than 4 Ys

* *

Rags and I went over the questionnaire on physical health. 'Don't you think I am too young for this?' I asked.

'Do you know young men are dying of heart attack? As young as twenty-eight? Anyway, you make an investment in health from the time you realize that you can lose it. Bad habits start when your mother overfeeds you processed milk products to make you a "chubby" baby.'

Much of the questionnaire included good suggestions. If I fell ill today, I would not know whom to consult. I decided to get a young family doctor. Maybe giving up smoking (I had done it almost every year!), cutting out fatty, oily foods, catching up on sleep, would all do me good.

'Will doing all this really make me live longer? Or will it just seem longer?' I asked Rags.

'The best thing is to die young,' he said, grinning sardonically. 'At the age of 100!'

'Hope I will see you touch 100,' I said, punching him in the arm.

'You look healthy to me. I'm sure you will make it to my hundredth birthday!' he joked.

The odds were against me. My mother died of cancer at forty-two, my father dropped dead of a heart attack, like his father before him, at fifty-two. I was the last one of a fragile crop.

'Long life is decided by both Nature and Nurture. Nurture is something you can control, to overcome the DNA lottery,' said Rags, reading my thoughts as usual. 'Go back and get everyone in your company to reflect on these questions. Impact the HR policy of your company.'

'The US and Canada carry only 10 per cent of the global burden of disease, yet these countries have 37 per cent of the world's health workers,' he continued. 'Africa, which has only 3 per cent of the world's health workers, carries 24 per cent of the global burden of disease. In Bhutan, there are many doctors from India and Myammar; overseas doctors are paid three times more than local doctors. Every step of life in poor Asian countries is taken under the twin shadows of poverty and inequality. 41 per cent of the world's poor are found in South-East Asia which houses 60 per cent of the world's population. 45 per cent of the population in India is young—the so-called demographic dividend. But young people with their incredible energy need proper jobs, opportunities to grow, a reasonable life. If they don't get it you have a revolution brewing on your hands.'

We opened the next tool, which was disguised as a folded apple.

* *

Experiential Attribute Matching

Experiential attribute matching involves importing feelings and ideas from an experience, like going to a movie or eating a durian.

Experiencing an event is totally different from thinking about it. Information from the five senses rush in, reflecting the ecstasy of the experience. Swimming in the river is totally different from thinking about it.

**

Rags reminisced, 'I remember a group in one of the innovation training programmes. We went for a turtle walk on a beach. We saw a large turtle alone on the sand. Inspired by this, one of the group came up with the idea that individuals in an organization should be allowed space to grow, without interference, in solitude. Yet another saw the slow and clumsy turtle and came up with an idea that postulated the exact opposite: let the organizational plan be clear and precise.'

**

Learn to capture dreams, visions and floating thoughts and synthesize them into your plans. Adapt to the environment, live each moment fully and never be a spectator. For spectators get nothing out of life, participants get everything. They live life in all its richness. The quality of their thoughts is rich, vibrant and in technicolour.

Action: Go to a movie together and import ideas from there to the problem.

* Thinking tools are the mathematics of innovation.
* Create a friendly atmosphere.

* Keep an open mind to receive feedback from within and outside.
* Stop smoking; don't add your own personal contribution to the polluting of the atmosphere.

**

Rags and I sat on the mountain slope and ate an apple as he took me through the five senses exercise.

**

This exercise helps you to unleash the power of the senses. Work life encourages you to be a one dimensional person. This reduces the power one can bring to an idea by accessing your five senses.

Take an apple. Hold it in your hand and experience it fully. Touch, feel, see, hear it while biting and tasting it. Apply the thoughts you have on this experience to the problem at hand.

This method was used by a leading financial institution to address the problem of how to attract and retain talent.

Seeing the apple made one of the groups think of the colour of passion. This was used to come up with the idea that individuals who are passionate enough about an idea to take the initiative and risk should be rewarded.

The sight of a rotten apple gave rise to the idea that negative elements should be identified and isolated.

The red and yellow apple reminded people about the sun and they said that HR policies should be like the rising sun.

Touching the apple reminded them of the womb and they felt that HR should be as safe as the womb.

The smoothness of the apple led them to say that career progressions should be smooth with no awkward bumps. 'Soft issues should be handled with a kind grandmother's touch,' said someone who remembered his first apple.

The smell of the apple drew attention to the need for a friendly, pleasant atmosphere.

The sounds made while eating an apple made people feel that HR policy should be crisp. The place of work should be quiet, with pleasant sounds.

The taste of the apple led to the idea that HR policy should be easy to digest and understand.

Thus, you can ask people to apply their sensory impressions to a problem and come up with solutions.

**

'The next world war will be fought over water,' said Rags as he handed me several sheets of paper. 'It's also been sent to your e-mail. Practise it and forward it to all your friends.'

**

52 Steps to Conserve Water

1. When washing dishes by hand, don't let the water run while rinsing. Fill one sink with wash water and the other with rinse water.
2. Check your sprinkler system frequently and adjust sprinklers so that only your lawn is watered and not the house, sidewalk or street.
3. Run your washing machine only when it is full and you could save 1000 gallons of water a month.
4. Install low-volume toilets.
5. Time your shower to keep it under five minutes. You will save up to 1000 gallons of water a month. Better still, use a bucket for your bath.

6. When you clean your fish tank, use the water you have drained on your plants. The water is rich in nitrogen and phosphorus, providing you with a free and effective fertilizer.

7. Put food colouring in your toilet tank. If it seeps into the toilet bowl, you have a leak. It is easy to fix, and you can save more than 600 gallons of water a month.

8. Don't use running water to thaw food.

9. Grab a wrench and fix that leaky faucet. It is simple, inexpensive, and can save 140 gallons of water a week.

10. Do one thing each day that will save water. Even if savings are small, every drop counts.

11. When the kids want to cool off, use the sprinkler in an area where your lawn or plants need it the most.

12. Bathe your young children together.

13. Wash your car on the grass. This will water your lawn at the same time.

14. Drop that tissue in the trash instead of flushing it and save gallons every time.

15. Support projects that use reclaimed waste water for irrigation and other uses.

16. Use a hose nozzle and turn off the water while you wash your car and save more than 100 gallons of water.

17. Encourage your friends and neighbours to be part of a water-conscious community.

18. Water only as rapidly as the soil can absorb the water.

19. Select the proper size pans for cooking. Large pans require more cooking water than may be necessary.

20. Turn off the water while you shave and you can save more than 100 gallons of water a week.

21. When you give your pet fresh water, don't throw the old water down the drain. Use it to water your trees or

shrubs. If you accidentally drop ice cubes when filling your glass from the freezer, don't throw them in the sink. Drop them on a house plant instead.

22. Spread the message of reproductive health and discipline to keep the planet viable.

23. To save water and time, consider washing your face or brushing your teeth while in the shower.

24. While staying in a hotel or even at home, consider reusing your towels. Use thin towels that dry easily.

25. Retrofit all household faucets by installing aerators with flow restrictors to slow the flow of water.

26. Check for leaks around your pumps.

27. Use the garbage disposal in the sink sparingly. Compost instead and save gallons of water every time.

28. Check your water meter and bill to track your wastage usage.

29. Wash your produce in the sink or a pan that is partially filled with water instead of running water from the tap.

30. Use a layer of organic mulch around plants to reduce evaporation and save hundreds of gallons of water a year.

31. Use a broom instead of a hose to clean your driveway or sidewalk and save 80 gallons of water every time.

32. If your shower can fill a one-gallon bucket in less than 20 seconds, then replace it with a water-efficient showerhead.

33. Collect the water you use for rinsing produce and reuse it to water house plants.

34. Divide your watering cycle into shorter periods to reduce runoff and allow for better absorption every time you water.

35. We are more likely to notice leaky faucets indoors, but don't forget to check outdoor faucets, pipes and hoses for leaks.

36. Teach your children to turn the faucets off tightly after each use.

37. Before you lather up, install a low-flow showerhead. They are inexpensive, easy to install, and can save your family more than 500 gallons of water a week.

38. Encourage your school system and local government to help develop and promote a water conservation ethic among children and adults.

39. After using your toilet, make sure the toilet flapper does not stick open and lead to wastage of water.

40. If your toilet was installed prior to 1980, place a toilet dam or bottle filled with water in your toilet tank to cut down on the amount of water used for each flush. Be sure these devices do not interfere with operating parts.

41. Wash clothes only when you have a full load and save up to 600 gallons of water.

42. Leave lower branches on trees and shrubs and allow leaf litter to accumulate on top of the soil. This keeps the soil cooler and reduces evaporation.

43. More plants die from over-watering than from under-watering. Be sure only to water plants when necessary.

44. Cook food in as little water as possible. This will also retain more of the nutrients.

45. Turn the water off while you shampoo and condition your hair and you can save more than 50 gallons of water a week.

46. Bathe your pets outdoors in an area in need of water.

47. Keep a bucket in the shower to catch water as it warms up or runs. Use this water to flush toilets or water plants.

48. When you are washing your hands, don't let the water run while you lather.

49. Soak your pots and pans instead of letting the water run while you scrape them clean.

50. Group plants with the same watering needs together to get the most out of your watering time.
51. While fertilizers promote plant growth, they also increase water consumption. Apply the minimum amount of fertilizer needed.
52. Turn off the water while you brush your teeth and save 4 gallons a minute. That's 200 gallons a week for a family of four.

52 Easy Ways to Save Money and the Planet

If you follow all, or even just some of the following money saving tips, you'll be surprised at just how much money you'll save every month. So please don't discount any of these tips: the actions may seem small and insignificant but when you add them all up, the money you save in energy and water is a nice chunk of change.

Plus, when you conserve energy and water you're also helping save our natural resources which makes you feel even better.

1. Turn the lights off when you're not in the room.
2. When a light bulb goes out, replace it with a compact fluorescent (CFL).
3. During the heat of the day, close the shades.
4. In the winter, open the shades.
5. In the summer, do not keep the air conditioning below 24°C.
6. Enroll in a money saving plan with your utility company, if available, to use the majority of energy at off-peak hours. (Ok, this technically doesn't save energy, but it does save you money!)
7. Unplug small appliances when they are not in use.
8. Use fans instead of turning down the air conditioning.

9. When you are done with the computer for the day, shut it off.
10. Plug your TVs, DVD players, game systems and computers in surge protector power strips and then shut them off when not in use.
11. Replace outdoor and landscape lights with solar lighting.
12. Instead of buying bottled water, put a filter on your tap water, boil it if required and use re-usable bottles or pitchers.
13. Drop the tissue into the trash, instead of flushing and save gallons of water every time.
14. When doing the laundry, only wash full loads.
15. Instead of throwing away unused water or ice, save it to water your plants.
16. When it rains, turn off your sprinklers and drip systems for a few days.
17. If you live in hot climates, do not have a lawn.
18. Water your plants and lawn at night (if you absolutely must have a lawn).
19. Landscape with only native plants so you do not have to water them.
20. Turn the water off when brushing teeth.
21. Only let the shower run for a few minutes when waiting for the water to heat up.
22. Use cloth towels instead of paper towels.
23. Don't wash your car that often.
24. When washing your car, do not let the hose run. Instead, fill a bucket and use that water for cleaning.
25. Buy concentrated cleaning products.
26. Always use cold water to wash clothes (yes, even when using regular detergent).
27. Run your dishwasher only when it is full.

28. Install low volume toilets. Use less water.
29. Don't use running water to thaw food.
30. Install a low-flow showerhead and bathe young children together.
31. To speed up the heating of the shower, turn one bathroom faucet on to the 'hot' position and run this until the shower turns warm.
32. Purchase recycled paper products.
33. Properly inflate your tires.
34. Instead of idling, shut your car engine off.
35. Go easy on the brakes when driving.
36. Avoid drag on your car.
37. If you're in the market for a new car, try and buy a hybrid or purchase one that gets at least 20 km/litre.
38. When you're in the market for new appliances, buy only energy efficient ones.
39. Purchase a programmable thermostat.
40. If you're in the market to buy a new computer, buy a laptop instead of a desktop.
41. If you're in the market for a new water heater, buy a tankless water heater.
42. Buy products with minimal packaging.
43. Buy local food when possible from village markets.
44. Combine errands so you reduce driving.
45. Walk, ride public transport or bike as often as you can.
46. Ask your employer to let you telecommute/work from home at least one day per week.
47. Clean the air-conditioning filters once a month during the summer.
48. Change your car's air filter when dirty.
49. Use timers for outdoor lights so they stay off during the day.
50. Reuse as many items as you can.

51. Replace leather with other materials like cloth.
52. Eat less meat, earn merit.

**

'Be the invisible traveller,' said Rags. Wherever we went, we carried a garbage bag. There have been instances of huge forest fires caused by a cigarette not stubbed out properly. Rags passed me a yellow post-it slip. It said:

> Take nothing but pictures
> Kill nothing but time
> Leave nothing but footprints

'There is so much we have discussed. What should I do for maximum impact?' I asked.

'Practise it. Then talk to your team and share it. Get your company to implement these ideas. Start ripples,' said Rags.

The takin is Bhutan's national animal. It was created by the Divine Madman, Lama Drupka Kinley. Rags quoted him: 'I believe in Lamas when it suits me. I use fair and foul words for mantras. It is all the same. My meditation practice is girls and wine and I do whatever I feel like strolling around in the Void.'

I loved the Divine Madman! We had so many in India.

Having made a meal of a whole cow, followed by a whole goat, he put the head of the goat on the cow's skeleton and commanded it to rise, which it did, then proceeded to graze, which is a good example of attribute matching.

One can also import ideas from a fan to create a revolutionary chair. Or apply ideas from a supermarket to build a revolutionary bus.

Bhutan has 165 species of mammals, including the Himalayan black bear, many types of deer and monkeys, and the elusive golden langur. The Royal National Park on Bhutan's central south border with India has tigers, leopards, rhinos and elephants.

In the upper Himalayan region you find yaks, rare blue sheep and the snow leopard. Bird watchers come to see rare species of birds. Porbijika Valley attracts the migratory black-necked crane. These birds have an elaborate mating ritual and they mate for life. Some other migratory bird species seen here are ospreys, waders and a wide variety of ducks besides snow pigeons, rose finches, accentors and various pheasants. You can also spot minivets, barbets, sunbirds, warblers, cuckoos and yuhinas. At high altitudes you can see the raven, the Himalayan griffon and the hammergeyer lazily riding the air currents in search of prey. More commonly visible are the blue whistling thrush, chattering yellow-billed magpies, choughs and many other species.

'Animals are also part of our world, they need kindness and love. But people treat them differently depending upon their commercial use,' Rags said. 'A farm in Belarus has 150,000 minks. They are beautiful, white, furry creatures, tumbling playfully over each other. But they are being reared to be killed to produce 150,000 pelts, fur coats to be worn by very rich women. On the other hand, Hamburg's famous Alster swans are collected during the winter and taken to special quarters where they are fed and cared for till spring. Kenyan villages protect their plantations by the humming of bees, which elephants are terrified of. Lucy King of Oxford University discovered this. The fences are connected to apiaries; the bees start buzzing when an elephant trips a wire.'

As we walked through the untamed jungle, we talked about wild ideas.

* *

Working with Wild Ideas

A germinal idea requires the sanctuary of a mindspace that is totally nurturing. It requires a space to grow so that its wildness is not nipped in the bud. Who knows which weed will become the coffee bush? Let the wilderness flourish in a totally non-threatening atmosphere. Let the ideas grow high and tall. Leave all pruning for later. New ideas need to play freely, with no discipline. Suspend judgment, postpone reaction, extend effort.

Hindustan Lever has its innovation centers. Cognizant has budgets for its mavericks and no 'stop' signs within those budget allocations. Many companies have innovation departments that coordinate this.

* *

'Ask all the participants to make an impossible wish: zero cost, zero rejections or double productivity. Then proceed to tame the wish bit by bit, using the innovation tools already learnt, like 6M,' Rags suggested. 'This process can be extended as you learn all the tools. So go ahead and spend time setting impossible goals and developing wild ideas.'

'Let us toss around a few wild ideas,' he challenged me.

'What about zero—which Indians discovered, without which all mathematics would have been impossible?' I said.

'Einstein?' asked Rags.

'Yes, so zero inventory, zero cost, zero manpower . . .' I suggested.

'Good. Any company would become profitable by moving towards this. Today with outsourcing, many companies are working towards zero manpower. Mechanization and the use of robots are doing the same thing. When you start with a wild idea, you first rescue the usable part of it and then tame the rest, bit by bit.'

'Like taming a bad habit, bit by bit!' I said.

Rags looked at me seriously and said, 'The thing about addictions—smoking, alcohol, drugs—is you cannot tame them bit by bit. You just have to stop, and go cold turkey!'

'To start with, you need to protect wild ideas in a mental sanctuary, like a tiger in a game sanctuary,' he continued. 'For instance, the Tibetans believe in seven Beyuls, hidden valleys scattered throughout the Himalayas and chosen by Guru Padmasambhava to remain havens of tranquillity and serve as safe refuge for followers of Buddhism during times of turmoil and threatening calamities. There are several valleys in Bhutan that live in a time warp even today, ready for the time they will be called upon to act as the vaults for the culture of humanity. Indeed it is this strong sense of destiny that has been imbued in the psyche of the nation since its birth in the fifteenth century, that is responsible for the extremely wary and cautious stance it has adopted while engaging the global world of today.'

I pondered for a while on wild, way-out ideas that have been proved successful.

In a recent survey, 81 per cent of Indian businessmen said that they owe their success to jugaad. This is a uniquely Indian word for the kind of innovation that allows Indians to 'somehow' manage their business in spite of lack of resources. The one virtue that brides and entrepreneurs alike are urged to embrace in India is to 'somehow adjust'. This creates the need for jugaad which has now found its way into Wikipedia. Instead of complaining about lack of R&D facilities, Indians have invented the $2500 car, the $800 electrocardiogram, the $24 water filter, the handheld simputer and the Android tablet computer Akash.

Jugaad is what Punjabi mechanics do when they cannibalize vehicles to create a cart which moves with a diesel engine. Or a diesel irrigation pumpset mounted on a steel frame. Punjabi farmers also use old washing machines to make lassi. Jugaad is about improvisation, being low cost, using anything at hand and just learning to 'manage' and somehow move, to inch forward. This jugaad way, which grew out of necessity, is the bottom of the pyramid's 'never say die' message to the world. Anil Ambani of Reliance says the way forward is innovation, not invention—preferably on a shoestring budget.

Look at the Honey Bee Foundation which promotes rural innovations. Washing clothes using an exercise cycle, for instance. Or consider Nitish Shetty of Bangalore, who said that an automated garbage sort-and-mould machine could increase the efficiency of garbage disposal and recycling. Or Apurva Bhandari of Sankalp Taru in Hyderabad or P.K. Pillai of Mumbai, who are building a modified cycle rickshaw to make it more efficient. Anita Ahuja trained rag pickers to collect garbage which is turned into designer hand bags under the brand name 'Conserve'.

Wild ideas and impossible goals need to have a 'Do or Die' feeling and passion attached to them. Like Gandhiji and his army of nameless millions, pursuing the impossible goal of 'Poorna Swaraj' or total freedom. The inspired surge that put Shivaji's 'mountain rats' on the path to victory is what is needed in a successful innovation. Start building the bridge from an impossible wild idea and tame it to become domesticated. Few wild ideas escape our internal censor board.

There is a stern censor board which evaluates all new ideas. The more impossible or different the idea is, the stronger the disapproval of the censor board. The harsh voices of our childhood gate-keepers, parents, teachers and elders succeed in suppressing all but the tamest ideas.

As Gary Zukov says in *The Dancing Wu Li Masters*, 'The importance of nonsense can hardly be overstated. The more clearly we experience something as "nonsense", the more clearly we are experiencing the boundaries of our own self-imposed cognitive structures. "Nonsense" is that which does not fit into the pre-arranged patterns we have superimposed on reality . . . Nonsense is nonsense only when we have not yet formed the point of view from which it makes sense.'

It helps to realize that ideas which are immediately accepted by the censor board are probably 200 years old and totally bereft of originality. We need to silence this censor board within our own minds, during the idea generation phase. At any given time there is a storm of thoughts whirling through our minds. Thoughts which need to be rescued and recorded without evaluating them at that time.

Are these statements nonsense?

'If glass is a fragile material, the ship can float' is about launching a ship with a bottle of champagne.

'If the wings ice up, the word is abbreviated' is about a skywriting plane that returns to base early because of weather problems.

'If the teeth are sharp, the ground shakes' is about using a chain saw to cut down a massive tree.

They seem absurd at first, devoid of meaning. But considered from another point of view, they make complete sense.

Think of the great Picasso who looked at the handlebar of a bicycle and created the sculpture of a bull with horns. He also said, 'Every act of creation is first of all an act of destruction.'

'There are some things that are so serious you have to laugh at them'—Niels Bohr

'We don't see things as they are; we see things as we are' —Anais Nin

---

Ishita Khanna of Spiti Ecosphere has developed eco-tourism, making many homes into bed-and-breakfasts in a distant village in the mountains, while creating a health product from the orange seabuckthorn berry which grows there.

Selco Solar lighting brought solar lighting to 120,000 homes in fifteen years, a single light per rural family at the cost of Rs 6 per day. 'No Excel sheet economics,' says Harish Hande of Selco, Bangalore. Poor people can pay and they can maintain technology. They wanted light for two hours in the morning to milk the cows. A solar panel made by Tata BP costs Rs 15,000. A Karnataka topper in the tenth standard studied with solar lighting. Families from Sonamhalli village who earn around Rs 1600 a month bought a Rs 9500 solar lighting system. Earlier they spent Rs 210 on candles and kerosene every month.

Ramachandra Gowda in Kolar, Karnataka installed 5000 bio-sand filters costing Rs 800 each, each filter providing clean drinking water for five families.

Rags said, 'Many people wonder what they can do in their individual capacity. But everything starts with you. Why think about how the whole country can be cleaned up? Just keep your own doorstep clean—but don't dump your garbage on your neigbhour's doorstep!'

'Like Rotary International is about to kick the polio virus out of this world, by vaccinating one child at a time, so that no child is left unreached,' I said. 'During 2011 there was only one child detected with polio in India.' In the last year there have been no polio cases in India.

'How come you know so much about Rotary and polio?' asked Rags curiously.

'My Dad was a Rotarian and would bicycle to distant places (no cars could go there) to make sure the vaccine was administered.'

'Are you a Rotarian?' asked Rags.

'I am too busy, too young,' I said.

'Rubbish!' said Rags. 'Join when you go home.'

I could see Rima and myself playing with the babies in the polio vaccination booth.

Metaphors

Metaphors could also be applied to gain fresh perspectives on a situation under analysis, Rags said. A metaphor is a term or phrase that is applied to another, unrelated term or phrase to create a nontraditional relationship. For example, 'all the world's a stage'.

Metaphors can be used to examine various situations. For example, an organizational environment might be the topic of analysis. One might ask, 'How do people in my organization resemble animals in a jungle? How do different animals manage their interactions with each other and how do we translate them into the different leadership styles that are used?' Answering these queries might allow new insights into the situation.

Rags listed the procedures for using metaphors for innovation:

1. Identify the issue you would like to innovate on, like 'How to make customers your raving fans?'
2. Ask each member of the group to record their feelings about movies.
3. Experiential metaphor may include having the group go for a movie.
4. Apply these ideas to the problem using force-fit and record all ideas.

'Go to the root of things. Turn that upside down. Instead of treating sickness develop health. Instead of fighting against war, develop friendship and peace. Instead of selling to customers, make customers sell for you!' Rags said.

'For instance, consider a tree as a metaphor of growth in your company,' he continued. 'Identify the processes of the tree.'

I quickly listed the processes, excited by my fluency:

1. Spreading branches
2. Birds that come to eat fruits
3. The flowers that attract bees
4. The seeds scattered by the birds to create new trees
5. The oxygen given out by the green leaves
6. The people who come to sit in the shade.

'What about the selfless nature of the tree, which does everything for others?' asked Rags impishly.

'Maybe my company should sincerely consider how to serve our clients and make them prosperous,' I said reflectively.

'Maybe you should develop the same attitude to suppliers, the public and shareholders,' he countered.

I remembered the time when all our neighbours had complained about the noise of our generators. I used to hate them for interfering with production. Maybe we needed to work on some dust and noise reducing processes.

'The branches made me think of a network of cottage industries who could take over some of our simpler processes at lower cost,' I said.

'The birds?' he challenged.

'Well, the birds could be graduate students from our best universities interning with us.'

'The flowers?'

'If the flowers are lovely they will attract the bees naturally, so if we make our product more customer-centric, the customers will beat a path to our door, fight to buy our product!'

'Wow! Wow!' he chuckled. 'You've got it, man! Your guru Michael Porter said: "Innovation is the central issue in economic prosperity." Innovation is critical to our country or any country. But no one is serious about it.'

Sirius had been growing totally bored with our conversations. He was tugging insistently at my shirt. I silenced him with a chocolate biscuit.

'Chocolate is bad for dogs,' I could hear Rima admonishing me when I tried to feed Coco, her spoilt supercilious little Lhasa Apso, whose back end I could not tell from the front end. Rima loved Coco so much. Sometimes I felt that the way to her heart was through Coco.

Rags gave me a little note which said, 'A wish list for innovation.'

**

A Wish List for Innovation

1. The government could play a major role in making innovation a key factor in economic leadership. There should be a Department of Innovation in the Central government with units in all State governments. The National Innovation Council is a good starting point. Members of Parliament should be trained in thinking tools and innovation.

2. Industry bodies like CII should set up innovation centres.

3. IIM Ahmedabad has a centre for Innovation, Incubation and Environment. All universities should have this.

4. Anna University in Chennai has an innovation centre. There is space and a need for hundreds of such centres, especially in academic institutions.

5. The Society for Innovation and Development (SID) at the Indian Institute of Science (IISc), Bangalore interacts with commerce and industry. This organization helps companies by providing them with incubators for new ideas. However, much more needs to be done.

6. Innovators should be honoured with national awards. Indian companies should have better facilities for filing patents for innovations and inventions. Many young inventors fall by the wayside because the patenting procedure is so expensive, time consuming and complicated. The government should have a more enabling attitude to protect the nation's wealth of ideas.

7. The educational system should be based on developing creative and innovative thinking. Thinking tools and methodologies should be part of the syllabus.

8. All technical institutions should have innovation and creativity taught as a subject. Companies should recruit innovative people and support them through the process of development. Textbooks on innovation and creativity should be written.

9. Companies should have CIOs (Chief Innovation Officers).

10. All induction programmes in organizations should include creativity and innovation.

11. The new trend in business is that people do not stay in jobs over a lifetime. An intensive programme to awaken organizational innovativeness and the possibility of enrolling new employees as organizational change agents should be presented early in the process.

12. The challenge facing leaders is on how to turn an outsider into an insider. Comfort and belonging is an important part of the climate of innovation. Entering a team mid-stream is tough. Handholding by management, especially by the human resources department, is essential.

13. Attention needs to be paid to the improved use of formal approaches to innovation. Information about innovation is not enough. Theoretical knowledge of innovation does not have an impact unless it is used practically. Top management support and organizational will are key to achieving the use of innovation processes and tools.

14. In India, there is a need to break the communication barrier by producing simple, local language materials, since the pressure on companies for immediate commercial returns is high.

**

'If the Government of India and the prime minister had the political will to do this, India would be the innovation capital of the world!' Rags enthused.

'What should I do with this?' I asked, goggling at Rags.

'Write about it in your local newspaper. Talk to your CEO, present this to your local MLA. Start doing some of the simplest things on the list. Like starting an innovation club for kids in the neighbourhood. Talk about it at your local Rotary club. Tweet about it, start a discussion on Facebook. Contact CEOs and HR heads of local corporates.'

'Do you want me to give up hopes of having a life?' I asked.

'If you do all this you may really get a life,' he said. 'Because true happiness is in helping others and changing the world, leaving your footprints on the sands of time, dude!'

There was a full moon in the sky. When Mom was alive we always had dinner on the terrace to celebrate the full moon.

Rags handed me a silver-grey folder.

**

The moon

When the moon sets, people say that the moon has disappeared; and when the moon rises, they say that the moon has appeared. In fact, the moon neither goes nor comes, but shines continually in the sky. The Buddha is exactly like the moon: he neither appears nor disappears; he only seems to do so, out of love for the people that he may teach them.

People call one phase of the moon a full moon, they call another phase a crescent moon; in reality, the moon is always perfectly round, neither waxing nor waning. The Buddha is precisely like the moon. In the eyes of humans, the Buddha may seem to change in appearance, but, in truth, the Buddha does not change.

The moon appears everywhere, over a crowded city, a sleepy village, a mountain, a river. It is seen in the depths of a pond, in a jug of water, in a drop of dew hanging on a leaf. If a man walks hundreds of miles the moon goes with him. To men the moon seems to change, but the moon does not change. The Buddha is like the moon in following the people of this world in all their changing circumstances, manifesting various appearances; but in essence he does not change.

All aspects of desire are impermanent and uncertain. Their loss causes suffering. If a person speaks and acts with a good mind, happiness follows him like a shadow.

If a diver is to secure pearls, he must descend to the bottom of the sea, braving all dangers of jagged coral and vicious sharks. So man must face the evils of worldly passion if he is to secure the precious pearl of enlightenment.

To be a trainer of elephants one must possess five qualifications: good health, confidence, diligence, sincerity of purpose and wisdom. Human desires are endless like a man drinking salt water.

[from *The Teaching of Buddha—Bukkyo Dendo Kyokai*]

* *

The moonlight touched the bubbling water of the Pa-chu and I was filled with silent happiness.

*

The Crawford Blue Slip

This is one of the simplest, yet very effective, creativity generation techniques. It can be used to collect a large number of ideas in a short time. Because the ideas are recorded and shared without the name of the originator, people feel more comfortable about expressing ideas and there is less concern that their ideas will not be considered as useful.

Procedure for Use

Each person receives a stack of blue slips. The leader presents a statement in 'how to' form; for example: 'How can our company improve its service to its customers?' Persons are then urged to write as many answers as possible within a five-minute period. Each answer is recorded on a separate blue slip. Next, the slips are collected and sorted; related ideas are grouped. Then they can be evaluated and regrouped, according to categories related to impact, originality, cost etc.

Example for Use

C.C. Crawford, originator of the technique, gives the example of gathering twenty people to define the requirements for a new industrial sealant. They wrote independently on five sub-targets:

1. Identify customers
2. Identify experts
3. Suggest members for a project management team
4. Identify possible constraints and limitations
5. Identify critical success factors

They then formed groups to sort and evaluate the ideas and decide upon a product definition. Their suggestion was adopted by the management and within days the product was in a prototype state, significantly reducing product development time.

Bug-list Technique

According to Hendry Petroski, author of *The Evolution of Useful Things*, inventors share the feeling of being driven by a real or perceived failure of existing things or processes to work as well as they might. Fault-finding with the world around them and disappointments with the inefficiencies with which things are done appear to be common traits among inventors. According to Marvin Camaras, an inventor quoted in the same book, 'Inventors tend to be dissatisfied with what they see around them . . . maybe they're dissatisfied with something they're actually working on or with an everyday thing . . . they say this is a very poor way of doing it.' The bug-list technique was developed to capitalize on this tendency of faulting things around us—to lead to corrective action.

Procedure for Use

1. The group is asked to identify things that irritate or 'bug' them. Each person is asked to identify five or ten bugs.
2. Then the list is consolidated to identify the bugs common to most persons.
3. The group is led through the list and asked to vote.
4. Then the group brainstorms ways to resolve the bugs.

Examples for Use

Bug	Solution
'That wretched bookmark fell out of my book again!'	Post-it slip
'Drat! I nicked myself again. This happens every time I change blades.'	Electric razor
'Where did I put those extra batteries?'	Solar powered appliances

'I hate paying a tax accountant to prepare my income tax report.'	Tax preparation software

Identify the bugs in your product or process and look for a solution.

*

'Do you know 400 million people are afflicted by mental illness?' asked Rags.

'Are you talking about the Chinese millionaires who are committing suicide?'

There was a recent Chinese study that showed that among the extremely wealthy, suicide was the cause of 23.6 per cent of deaths between 2008 and 2010. Needing the help of alcohol or sleeping tablets tells the inside story of material success. The true definition of happiness could be 'a good night's sleep, every night'. The singleminded pursuit of monetary wealth can cut out all other sources of wealth—family, sports, music, books and friends.

'No, I am talking about the malaise that affects everyone: from schoolchildren who commit suicide because they did not get good grades to housewives who are bored out of their wits after having brought up their children and are now at a loose end, because neither the kids nor the husband have time for them.'

'What about burnt-out software engineers?' I butted in.

'What worries me is the way more and more people are choosing inappropriately aggressive ways of dealing with conflict,' said Rags. 'A twenty-one-year-old, Oscar Ramino Osteya, shot at the White House, hoping to kill President Barrack Obama. He said he was "agitated about the federal government"! A Korean teenager killed his mother for expecting higher grades from him and hid her body in the bedroom for eight months. The bodies of mutilated and abused girl children found in a drain outside a house in Nithari, Uttar Pradesh, speaks of mounting levels of depravity, perversion and unhappiness.'

'We need to develop positive emotions like love, compassion, courage, laughter and wonder in our lives,' I said, 'and work at uprooting negative emotions like anger, lust, greed and jealousy.'

'What the sad world needs is an attitude of giving. The fastest way to be happy is to help others,' said Rags.

'The rich who have so much, should give,' I suggested.

'Everyone, even the poorest, can give,' Rags corrected me. 'Here is what the Buddha says: There are seven kinds of offering which can be practised by even those who are not wealthy. The first is the physical offering. This is to offer service by one's labour. The highest type of this offering is to offer one's own life. The second is the spiritual offering. This is to offer a compassionate heart to others. The third is the offering of eyes. This is to offer a warm glance to others which will give them tranquillity. The fourth is the offering of countenance. This is to offer a soft countenance with a smile to others. The fifth is the oral offering. This is to offer kind and warm words to others. The sixth is the seat offering. This is to offer one's seat to others. The seventh is the offering of shelter. This is to let others spend the night at one's home. These kinds of offering can be practised by anyone in everyday life.'

This was quite an eye-opener to me.

'Create a tomorrow file,' Rags suggested. 'Whatever can't be done today, may become possible tomorrow.

Leonardo da Vinci had drawings of cars, satellites and submarines in his notebooks long before science could support their production.'

He handed me a sheet of blue paper.

**

Create a Sanctuary for Ideas

Once a new product idea germinates, time and space is needed for participants to grow and develop that idea. The immediate reaction is to remove all elements that make the product new and different. Most groups will dash in to protect familiar aspects of the product. The sanctuary is a tool that can be used to protect all germinal ideas. It involves inventing or shaping the future together in a protected environment. It is a radical new approach.

Sanctuary 1 is used to protect an impossible idea from immediate destruction. The tool used here is to protect the idea. Allister Pilkington's discovery of plate glass started when he noticed the grease forming on dishwater. Poured on water, glass would be perfectly flat. This idea was protected and various liquids were considered in place of water. Finally the process worked when molten glass was poured on liquid tin! But the original idea had to be protected long enough for the final idea to emerge.

Fred Smith, in his final year of college, had a wild idea— parcels could be delivered overnight using a private airline system with a centralized hub. He dreamt about it as he was flying sorties during the Vietnam war. Today, thanks to his preservence in protecting a wild idea till it could be tamed to work, we have a very profitable Federal Express.

Example: Parking on a busy road becomes a problem due to overcrowding and lack of adequate parking space. Wild idea: drivers with license plates ending with odd and even numbers could be encouraged to drive only on alternate days.

This can lead to the idea of providing parking spots for different cars on different days of the week. So each car would receive special facilities only on certain days of the week. This would encourage car pooling and a shift of leisure time activities to times when the congestion is less.

The impossible helps to put a fence around an idea which is impossible, thus allowing it to develop without immediate attack.

Sanctuary 2 is very similar to attribute matching. They help us to put together dissimilar ideas and expert solutions from different fields. If you would like to get fresh ideas on education, compare it to a motor car. The attributes of a motor car are:

1. It moves
2. It should be regularly filled with petrol
3. It can carry people
4. It provides a good view of the country
5. It has four wheels

Applying some of the ideas to education will ensure that we get a whole group of creative ideas, like an educational programme should put different types of people together in close proximity (as in a motor car) and enable them to share ideas in a time bubble away from others. Another idea might be that education should provide regular inputs from an outside source (like petrol), maybe ideas from people in government or agriculture, or nuclear physics.

Education till high school is free in Bhutan. But education for what? Many school graduates do not want to stay in their villages.

They are unhappy and frustrated. India has the same problem. How can one improve the villages so that the revolution of rising expectations created by television can be met? How can villages be made more attractive to the young?

Perhaps including education in skills that will keep people employed in the villages is the solution.

**

'Lack of education is the greatest obstacle to growth. Illiteracy establishes a lifelong tyranny, pushing families into poverty. Let us think about how to develop our educational systems,' said Rags.

'Why can't educated, unemployed mothers be pulled into the system? Today it is so difficult to be a teacher,' I suggested. 'Why can't we have cottage schools, where mothers teach a few kids in their own homes?'

'Let's try a thinking tool,' said Rags. 'We need to be very humble when we look for ideas. Dr Edwin Land's daughter wished she could have pictures of her birthday party immediately. Land thought of a film that could develop itself on the spot and gave the world Polaroid.'

**

Sanctuary 3 is a tool to generate alternativeness. When a system is working well, as a matter of routine it should be used to encourage to think of ten alternative ways of doing it better. This is an important and interesting tool to prevent stagnation.

Imagine a company caught by high cost during a downturn. Now develop five ways to reduce costs. For example:

- Ask people to work for three days a week
- Encourage people to take an unpaid sabbatical

- Encourage working from home or telecommunicating
- Get vendors to supply completed parts and components to the assembly line. This will eliminate the need for stores and inventory
- Get customers to sell to other customers for a small fee

'Every company has before it a hundred alternative solutions,' said C.K. Prahalad. 'The trick is to get people to connect to each other with their ideas, so that each can build on others' ideas.' Newton himself said, 'If I saw further it is because I stood on the shoulders of giants.' New ideas often stall because so many of us put a fence around ideas. Sharing it with others, playing ping pong with them, snowballing them in brainstorming could be the best way of developing the ideas.

To collaborate, we need to listen lovingly, assuming value in the wildest idea. Appreciation enables others to open their deepest thoughts to us. Helping others through a springboard will develop the wildest idea. Laughing at others, demanding the kind of precision impossible in a new idea, pulling rank and nagging can certainly prevent a great idea from getting implemented.

We just need to remember the Japanese proverb, 'None of us is as smart as all of us'. Many ideas grow better in the garden of a fresh, new mind.

**

We walked back to our campsite.

six

It was a misty morning, and I needed all my warm clothes. Rags's only concession to the climate was a colourful monkey cap. 'You create your own climate!' he said, grinning mockingly when he saw me all bundled up.

'What ideas do you have on improving the GNH by preserving and promoting the cultural heritage of your community?' he then asked.

'Why should people be happy?' I asked lightly, full of the joy of living.

'Happy people are peaceful and innovative people. Even the US Constitution's stated objectives include life, liberty and the pursuit of happiness,' he said.

'The "pursuit of happiness" somehow makes it sound like it's quite tough to catch it!' I retorted.

'Happiness is a God-given right. The pursuit of happiness suggests that you have to proactively chase it to get it. Perhaps that is not necessary. Contentment is the path to true happiness,' said Rags.

He handed me a red folder, saying, 'Here are some findings in a book on the subject by Arthur C. Brooks. Conservatives are twice as likely to be happy. Those married with stable families are happier. Religion makes people 82 per cent happier. Optimistic, productive people are more likely to be happy.'

'My mom always said contentment is superlative happiness!' I said.

'A University of Barcelona study indicates that nuts like almonds, walnuts and brazil nuts create higher level of serotonins in the brain. Now serotonin convinces your brain that you feel wonderful, even if you don't have any obvious reason to.'

'Well, we always eat peanuts with our beer Saturdays—and everyone feels great!' I said.

'Also, studies show that happiness leads to a long life, health, resilience and good performance,' said Rags, clinching the issue.

'Liberals are more pessimistic and less happy, he says.' I was reading from the paper. 'If you are giving away money, you can double your happiness. 90 per cent of employed Americans like their jobs. Only 11 per cent of those employed are unhappy. The prime minister of Bhutan Jigme Thinley says, "Happiness is about joyful birth and parenting, meaningful and satisfying labour, ageing with contentment and security and dying in dignified security."'

'What is your mother tongue?' Rags shot at me.

I put my tongue out and said 'Pink, like yours!' We both fell over laughing. 'Tulu,' I said, recovering.

'One of those ancient languages with no script? Do you speak it well?' he asked gravely.

'I speak it. How well, I don't know. My aunts from Mangalore say I speak it like English.' We both laughed.

'Preserving culture starts at home. The Bhutanese speak Dzongha at home and learn it at school together with English. Speaking your language to your children preserves culture like nothing else can. Cultural diversity is being destroyed as thousands of indigenous languages are being forgotten, when kids go to school and learn English,' Rags said.

'English is India's bridge to the world,' I pointed out. 'I love English myself, otherwise I would not have been able to move freely around the Tower of Babel our country is, with seventeen official languages and thousands of dialects.'

'Customs and traditions are preserved in the home,' said Rags. 'The Marathas who settled in Tanjore many years ago still speak their language and maintain their customs in their own corner of Tamil Nadu, where they are famous weavers and are called Pattu Nool or silk threads.'

'How did they manage this?' I asked curiously.

'Well, brides are always brought from their hometowns.'

I digested this. Then I sent Rima a text message.

> **Enku ninada bari preethi**

That's 'I like you very much' in Tulu.

I had still not posted the poems.

Sirius tugged at my hand calling me to play. 'Having a dog increases your lifespan,' I said as I tumbled on the grass with Sirius.

'You're right,' said Rags. 'AAT or animal assisted therapy which involves encounters with selected animals has had miraculous results in the treatment of depression, anxiety and schizophrenia. It is also used to help children with cerebral palsy. The unconditional love that animals give heals those suffering from bereavement and prevents suicide.'

'Why can't families do this?' I asked.

'No time,' said Rags simply, tossing a stick for Sirius to chase.

My cellphone beeped.

Enkula

said the sms from Rima. 'Me too.' I was stunned. How did she know Tulu?

We all spoke Tulu in our village. I remembered the three-day Nemas, the festival for the Goddess, where ancient stories were preserved as an oral tradition. Every year, 150 members of the Kanekaria family (that is, my family) still assembled to worship Dhoomavathy, the goddess of rain and clouds. I never thought the kids were interested, till one day I found a poem among my young nephew's papers, after he went away to the US and left behind his childhood in an old trunk. It revealed a sensitive soul we had never known:

My goddess

I went to my village
the night our goddess moves from her temple to her home
the whole village gathers while drummers, trumpeters play
she enters in spirit
painted bedecked masked artist
she plays with fire and knives
re-enacting age-old tales
I can't understand most of it
I am fascinated by all around me
the spirits, the villagers, the children, the tattooed village
    bad asses,

my grand dad, dad, grand mom, mom, grand uncles, great aunts
    deal with the goddess
they placate her, they get blessed by her, it's lovely how
    she protects us
all of us believe
in between
I went down to Nethravati
she's the river behind the village
a five-minute walk though thickets
feels like a jungle, all closed with trees narrow paths
I figure my way through
half afraid of mad dogs, snakes
and chance upon the river
she is spectacular
a mile wide and still as a mirror
the evening sun bounces off
her surface
it's cool
my mother's mother's mother's mother's family grew up by
    this river
my phone rings
gotta get back cause the goddess is coming back home
we welcome her back with many garlands
she blesses everyone again, she inspects home
everyone is there, entire family in a room
every year
with drums booming, pipes playing another worldly tune
the fire handler is trying to calm the goddess
fire in one hand, oil jug in another
minute by minute he feeds flames
from his never ending jug
soon it's all gonna end
the festivities will be over
we go back
to cities

but for one day
in a tiny Mangalorean village
going back as long as I can remember
we pay our respects as a family
I am so fortunate
thanks to our goddess

'Culture is more than language and handicrafts,' said Rags, smiling at me.

'But culture can also suppress the rights of groups. Like dowry and bride burning or sati,' I said. I remembered the pathetic kumkum-smeared hand prints of women anaesthetised with opium and forced to commit sati, so that generations of daughters-in-law could worship them; or dalit women paraded naked for defying a higher caste man or an 'untouchable' hung from a tree for looking at a 'high caste' woman bathing by the well. Yet, in 1905, the American President Grover Cleveland wrote, 'Sensible and responsible women do not want to vote.'

I opened Mom's book to one of my favourite poems 'Lost' which she had written about a friend who had married a merchant prince in Kalimpong.

Lost

He the prince
Had captured her
Enchanted by the flashing splendour
Of her tiger eyes
The mountain mist in her flyaway hair
And kept her captive
In his ancient home
On a lonely hill.
To be the presiding deity
Of his cool drawing room

With light reflecting listlessly
Through cobwebs
Hung over blind shuttered windows
He'd liked the tenor of her mind
Fine, sensitive, fresh from convent school.
So he'd brought her to his castle
To keep a count of knives and spoons
To oversee the pickles and preserves
And now . . .
Her eyes have lost
Their tiger gleam,
Her hair is a lank and listless brown
Her voice echoes lost worlds
She's a skeletal butterfly
Embalmed in blue diamond glass.
And he?
Fresh from a jaunt to distant lands
He says, 'She's lost her charm.'

Mom found the brightest girl in her class, tired and totally washed out after years of marriage. She had been left behind to guard the pumpkins and preserves on the family terrace. 'There is no use marrying your dream girl and then neglecting her—and complaining when she becomes a nightmare,' she had said.

We are happiest when basking in the unconditional positive regard of others. It may be part of a bouquet of related emotional states that embraces joy, pleasure, amusement, satisfaction, triumph and euphoria.

I would always keep Rima smiling, I promised myself silently.

Rags loved the poem. 'Your mom was a wordsmith and you take after her,' he said.

I glowed inside.

'Now, what is the way to help children learn their language and culture? Let us generate a few ideas to solve this problem. The Maori in New Zealand instituted "language nests" in which toddlers were immersed in the Maori language from a very young age. There has been a revival of practices and traditions and political assertiveness of ancient tribes. Cultural capital is something that cannot be ignored,' said Rags.

My thoughts were elsewhere. I still could not understand how Rima had replied in Tulu. Did she care enough to learn Tulu for my sake?

Rags pushed a folder into my hands.

**

Diversity Tool 1: Use the Naïve Resource

Invite a surgeon to be involved in a one hour session with a team of architects building a town hall. Invite a ten-year-old child to speak to the community on how to preserve the language. Invite the new recruits to talk to the HR team on induction training, on retention and fun in the workplace.

Company-wide innovation is not about nurturing solitary genius in sterile laboratories, but requires the bubbling enthusiasm of teams.

* Promote mutual understanding.
* Rediscover God.
* Do not use elevators when you can climb the stairs.

Diversity Tool 2: Alternative Views

Help participants appreciate the point of view of otherwise ignored groups and stakeholders. A holiday resort company setting up a resort in a pristine tribal area in Nagaland invites the local tribals to participate in a session examining ways to maintain the environment while involving them as employees and guides. There was an interesting session when one of the tribals took the role of a cricket (a small insect) in the jungle. The fragility of the ecosystem was brought home to the promoters.

* The rules for thinking are different from the rules for doing. Implementation is possible only with a clear foundation of rational thought and practical application.
* Help a team member when they are in distress.
* Set personal goals.
* Enroll in a Transcendental Meditation (TM) programme today.

Diversity Tool 3: Interns

Invite a student from a premier foreign university to work in the department. Encourage him/her to work on a burning issue. Involve him/her in an Innovation Spiral.

* Adopt Tent Thinking rather than Marble Palace Thinking.
* Keep things in the right place.
* Focus on now.
* Focus on your breathing. Take a deep breath, and then exhale slowly. Repeat a couple of times a day.

Bring Adbhutha or Wonder into the Organization

This is a very useful, feel-good emotion. Welcome wonder into your life. Celebrate the beauty of the stars and enjoy the wonder of the mountains. Greet the dawn and say goodbye to the sunset. The moonlight has been created to heal your wounds.

Sleep on the lap of Mother Nature and become a child again. Go on excursions with your team.

***

**

In Bhutan everything evokes Adbhutha. The beauty of the natural landscape flows into the beauty of the buildings. No licences are given unless the traditional architecture and painting is incorporated. A skilled painter can earn Rs 3000–4000 a day. Every building, even a shop, has the traditional murals and frescos on the front walls. The eight lucky signs are painted everywhere. 'Sometimes I feel there is too much colour,' said a world traveller we met at one of the camps. He told us about the instinctive nature of Bhutanese architecture.

'Chorten Kora is built along the lines of the great Bodhnath Stupa in Nepal. The replica was originally carved on a turnip. The turnip shrank quite a bit on its journey. So the design became much smaller. Painted pure white, an annual Kora festival is held here. People spend the whole night going round and round the chorten. This often becomes a chance to enjoy a romantic interlude or even finalize a wedding. There is a narrow passage that one can squeeze through to rid oneself of one's sins. This proves that most Bhutanese architects live by the faith that ideas should flow from the mind of the builder and not be bound by a blueprint. Most of the dimensions and decorations are supported by tradition,' said Rags.

'Pema Lingpa, a tenton who was born in a family of blacksmiths and carpenters is said to have created 100 termas or hidden treasures,' he continued. 'In Bumthang, there are thirteen disciplines listed in his writings:

1. Painting
2. Sculpture
3. Carving
4. Blacksmithing
5. Casting
6. Carpentry
7. Gold and silver melting
8. Weaving
9. Embroidery
10. Masonry
11. Leather work
12. Bamboo work
13. Papermaking

Commisioning a painting as a *jinda* is a pious act. Many thangkas, murals and painted statues may have been prepared with this purpose. Murals are painted on fine cloth; a paste of pepper and flour prevents termites.'

**

Action to bring Adbhutha into your life

* Be alone in silence with nature at the beginning and end of every day.
* Enjoy a walk among tall trees and green gardens.
* Plant seeds and saplings. Distribute them.
* Set apart time for prayer to praise God for His glorious creation.
* Set apart time to enjoy beauty.

**

I looked at a new folder that Rags had handed me as he was holding forth on thangkas and murals.

Turncoat

This is a technique, one aspect of which is to look at the opposite of what we want. For example, look at how to increase costs or how to reduce turnover or deposits, and then turn the points made upside down to arrive at how to reduce costs and increase turnover. People find it easier to be negative than to come up with a cost reduction technique. This technique can be combined with attribute matching.

For example,

Problem: How to reduce cost?

6M	How to Increase cost ↑	How to Decrease cost ↓
Men		
Materials		
Machines		
Methods		
Markets		
Money		

* Play devil's advocate—take the exact opposite view of the one you have been holding.
* Everyone should take responsibility and ownership.
* Write down your worries—and then let go.
* Learn to relax. Spend 20 minutes consciously relaxing each muscle of your body.

CAPS

The CAPS concept enhances and supplements the 4Ps of the marketing mix and has special significance in the marketing of services. The following connections may be considered.

1) **Price +** Consider the inconvenience that is caused to the customer. This could be loss of time, safety or loss of dignity. This adds to price.
2) **Place +** Access refers to the ease with which a service can be conveniently used.
3) **Promotion +** Promotion of services explore the many aspects of a service that are intangible.
4) **Product +** Service has far more dimensions than a product and can only be experienced, not touched or smelt.

Procedure for Use:

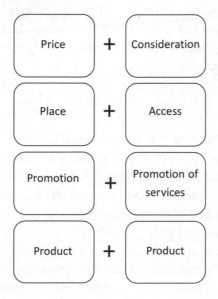

**

'Let us apply it to improve social capital,' said Rags. 'This means developing networks that make the community vital, warm and helpful. A rich man who has no social capital, could be a man who's found murdered in his antiseptic, sealed home, ten days later.'

'I often think that sometimes, in big cities, people live in their own tightly sealed bubbles,' I agreed. 'I have seen hundreds of people walking around a bleeding accident victim lying on the road.' I remembered how my friend Ajitha had died. She was studying architecture in a Bangalore college and had just returned for a holiday. Someone on a speeding motorbike hit her on a road where her family had lived for decades. She lay bleeding from her mouth and it was an hour before anyone took her to a hospital. After struggling for days on life support, she finally ended up in the government mortuary, only because no one had helped in that first critical golden hour.

Rags had handed me some sheets of paper; I looked through them.

**

Community vitality is the key to individual and family well-being. Whether it is prevention of crime or mental illness or sheer loneliness, community support can be an effective cushion against the anomie that besets modern life. Human beings are profoundly shaped by the communities within which they live, love, work, play and pray.

Successful communities or vital communities are cohesive, capable of acting together, able to develop and deploy resources. They provide social support, extend assistance to family, friends and neighbours. Cynicism and suspicion is less.

If someone abuses you, do not react in the same way. It is like spitting against the wind and the spit lands on your own face. Or like sweeping dust against the wind. Today many say, 'I hardly have time for myself, how can I worry about others' needs?'

In vital communities, everyone is their brother's keeper. Social networks are not a miracle cure or a panacea for all ills. But they are mankind's most important safety net for a happy, secure life.

52 Ways to Increase Social Capital

1. Organize a social gathering to welcome a new neighbour.
2. Join a Rotary club or a similar social action group.
3. Register to vote and do vote.
4. Support local merchants.
5. Volunteer your special skills to an NGO.
6. Donate blood (with a friend).
7. Start a community garden. Exchange plants and seeds.
8. Mentor someone of a different ethnic or religious group.
9. Surprise a new neighbour by making a favourite dinner— and include the recipe.
10. Record your parents' earliest recollections and share them with your children.
11. Plan a vacation with friends or family.
12. Avoid gossip.
13. Help fix someone's flat tyre.
14. Organize or participate in a sports league.
15. Join a book club.
16. Attend home parties when invited.
17. Become an organ donor or blood marrow donor.
18. Attend your children's athletic contests, plays and recitals.
19. Get to know your children's teachers.

20. Sing in a choir.
21. Get to know the clerks and sales people at your local stores.
22. Volunteer in your child's classroom or chaperone a field trip.
23. Join or start a baby-sitting cooperative.
24. Attend cultural functions and express appreciation for others.
25. Offer to shop for a sick neighbour.
26. Have family dinners and read to your children.
27. Go to temples (or a mosque, church or gurudwara) or walk outside with your children; talk to them about why it's important.
28. Take dance lessons with a friend.
29. Gather a group to clean up a local park or cemetery.
30. Say hello to strangers.
31. Log off and go to the park.
32. Ask a new person to join a group for a dinner or an evening.
33. Play host to a pot luck meal or participate in them.
34. Volunteer to drive someone.
35. Say hello when you spot an acquaintance in a store.
36. Play host to a movie night.
37. Exercise together or take walks with friends or family.
38. Assist with or create your town or neighbourhood's newsletter.
39. Start a group to discuss local issues.
40. Pick it up even if you didn't drop it—trash.
41. Join a project that includes people from all walks of life.
42. Sit on your veranda.
43. Be nice when you drive.
44. Make gifts of time.
45. Send a 'thank you' letter to the editor about a person or event that helped build community.

46. When inspired, write personal notes to friends and neighbours.
47. Organize a fitness/health group with your friends or co-workers.
48. Ask to see a friend's family photos.
49. Start a laughter club.
50. Help someone who least expects it.
51. Say 'thanks' to public servants: police, firefighters, doctors and nurses in government centres.
52. Open the door for someone who has his or her hands full.

**

'I was part of a "Save a life club" in Chennai, which was a civic movement started by a hospital to help accident victims. It reduced public apathy, taught first aid to traffic policemen, identified killer spots and developed a network of ambulances and hospitals,' I recalled.

'Great! Every city can do it,' said Rags.

*

Cultural vitality is defined as evidence of creating, disseminating, validating, and supporting arts and culture as a dimension of everyday life in communities. It belongs to us all—not just 'the arts community'.

The four dimensions of Cultural Vitality are:

(a) the presence of opportunities for participation,
(b) the level of participation in arts and cultural activity,
(c) the support for arts and cultural activity,
(d) the impact on communities and economies.

To maximize Cultural Vitality, conditions are ideal when there is:

- a mix of public and private operators (public, non-profit and commercial)
- a mix of formal and temporary settings (such as festivals, parades and markets)
- a mix of amateur and professional involvement in art- making in all forms
- when key organizations are recognized and supported as catalysts
- when diverse places exist for informal art-making and consumption
- when Internet capacity and use is maximized
- when the design of public spaces stimulates or supports cultural activity
- when arts and culture are embedded in formal education
- when culture is integrated into all general policies and plans
- when there is a high ratio of residents working as artists and cultural practitioners
- when there are places that facilitate audience access to cultural activity.

Creating a vital community and ensuring a development of culture is each individual's civic responsibility.

Excursion

Excursion helps bring fresh ideas from different fields into the group. The group is sent outside, maybe to a supermarket, and asked to focus on something which interests or intrigues them. Encourage the team to pick up objects and ideas. The participants in their enthusiastic mood are asked to apply their new experiences and objects to the problem.

Procedure for Use

1. Pick a product which you want to recreate for greater convenience, say a bus.

2. Visit a supermarket and write down the attributes of the experience: the fun, the convenience, the food, the social experience etc.
3. Apply these emotions and attributes to the design of the bus.
4. You may have a bus with low steps making it convenient for schoolchildren and senior citizens. The bus may provide seating to enhance social interaction. Computer terminals and movies could enhance the experience.

   * The best attitude for idea generation is to be relaxed but alert.
   * Write a little about the father's work to the kid. Say in writing, 'We are proud of your father.'
   * Learn to love and appreciate yourself.
   * Learn the healing power of laughter. Watch a crazy movie, recall a joke or read a funny book and laugh out loud.

Force Field Analysis

The name comes from the technique's ability to identify forces contributing to or hindering a solution to a problem, and can stimulate creative thinking in three ways:

1) To define what you are working towards (vision),
2) To identify strengths you can maximize, and
3) To identify weaknesses you can minimize.

   • At the centre of the sheet, write a statement of the problem you wish to solve.
   • Just below, at the left of the sheet, describe what the situation would be like in the worst case scenario, i.e. a catastrophe.
   • On the same line, at the right of the sheet, describe the ideal, or optimal, situation.
   • The centre position represents your current situation. On the right, describe the 'forces', tugging right now to move

the situation toward the ideal. Then describe on the left side the forces moving toward catastrophe.

The next step is to identify approaches that would improve the situation. Since the typical situation resembles a tug-of-war, use the following three approaches to move the centre line in the direction of the more desirable outcome:

* Identify things that would strengthen an already positive force.
* Identify things that would weaken an already negative force.
* Add new positive forces.

Springboard

There is a brainstorming technique, which was developed by George Prince, founder of Synectics and one of the pioneers of the creative thinking movement. This is a technique called developmental thinking, which is used to explore ideas which are attractive but not yet feasible.

In simple terms, if two people, A and B, are discussing an idea by A, B should in response identify three elements which he likes about the idea. This encourages A. B then goes on to give an itemized response on any specific concerns about the idea. The concerns should be specific and identify problem areas for A to solve. Instead of being adversaries on opposite sides of a problem, A and B become partners in growing the idea in a peaceful, nurturing climate.

There is a great deal of work done by thinkers on how to make the group climate more creative and less hostile. In developmental thinking, as the teachers at Synectics say, 'All potentially positive features of the ideas are identified and the deficiencies are used to give the direction for improvement, preserving the element of novelty while the idea is modified to make it feasible.' This process is a contrast to the conventional screening of ideas into 'good' and 'bad' after a typical brainstorming session, when novel ideas are likely to be screened out because they are not feasible.

* Yoga, meditation or any other form of stillness will ensure that you are in an ideal state for thinking fluently.
* Make watching a movie on TV an occasion: dress up, eat popcorn . . .
* Take responsibility for change.
* Balance your lifestyle. Devote equal time each week to work and fun.

Brain-writing Technique

The distinction in brain-writing, as opposed to brainstorming, is the generation of ideas individually and recording them on a piece of paper. The advantage over brainstorming is a reduction in the effect of dominating individuals. Brain-writing ensures that all participants have an equal opportunity to share their ideas.

As you share ideas, use the Springboard Technique and rotate the idea among participants with each person expanding and improving the idea. By the time the process is completed, everyone has ownership in the idea. The result is a more mature idea, ready to be implemented, compared to the results of brainstorming where the ideas are mostly immature.

Procedure for Use

1. The problem or opportunity is recorded at the top of a sheet of paper.
2. Participants record possible solutions on the sheet of paper.
3. The sheets of paper are collected and distributed randomly among participants. Each time the sheets are redistributed, care is taken to ensure that recipients never receive the same sheet twice.
4. The recipient of a sheet is asked to record three useful things about the idea.

5. The sheets are collected and redistributed and Step 4 is repeated.
6. The sheets are collected and redistributed and Step 4 is repeated.
7. The sheets are collected and redistributed. Recipients are then asked to respond to the question, 'What is missing from the idea: what would make it more useful?'
8. The sheets are collected and redistributed and Step 7 is repeated.
9. The sheets are then collected and redistributed for the final time. Recipients are asked, 'Assume that cost is not a constraint, what has to happen to make this idea work?'
10. The sheets are collected and typed up for review.

The approach normally produces sufficient information for each idea to be forwarded to management for evaluation.

Brainstorming Technique

Originated by Alex Osborn, brainstorming was designed to separate idea generation from idea evaluation. It has the objective of moving people into an atmosphere of a freewheeling thought process whereby ideas are stimulated through hearing others' ideas. The emphasis is on quantity of ideas, using the philosophy that quantity produces quality.

Procedure for Use

The following ground rules for effective brainstorming are recommended:

1. Pick a problem/opportunity where each person has the knowledge/motivation to contribute.
2. Define the problem in neutral terms rather than a preselected solution, e.g. 'How do we get this job done?' rather than 'How do we get this person or this group to do this job?'

3. Record the ideas on flip charts or large pieces of paper where everyone can see them.
4. Suspend evaluation or judgment until all ideas have been given.
5. Stretch for ideas.
6. When you think you've got all the ideas, go for another round, being even more outrageous in possible solutions.
7. Aim for quantity to help find quality.
8. Accept all ideas, even weak ones.
9. Encourage embellishment and building on ideas.

Wildest Idea Technique

The approach here is to move people out of their normal problem-solving modes, which are usually quite conservative, by asking them to try to come up with a 'wild' idea. An example was the discovery of radar, which was developed from the bizarre suggestion of a radio 'death-ray' for shooting down planes. Instead of rejecting the idea, someone used it as a stepping stone to formalize the concept of radar.

A paint company had a problem of peeling paint. During lunch break someone joked that it was best to 'Blow it up!' The idea was taken to the lab, where they found a chemical additive which would ensure that the paint could be peeled in large strips.

A scientist in a car company asked, 'Why paint cars? Why not use materials which do not require painting?'

*

'So, why not use stones and a rough finish without painting walls?' I asked.

'Bravo amigo!' said Rags, bowing deeply from the waist.

*

The approach is most useful when an impasse has been reached in problem solving or opportunity identification. Participants need to be jogged out of their mindset by considering things so remote or unusual that they change their normal frame of paradigm paralysis. It takes a while to get a group into the swing of generating wild ideas. Most of the ideas are impractical, but eventually a useful one emerges. It is usually one that couldn't be produced by one of the more conservative techniques.

Procedure for Use

1. The facilitator selects the first wild idea as a starting point and asks the group to build on the idea.
2. The group continues to explore variations or extrapolations of the wild idea.
3. Then the facilitator asks the group to try to find practical uses of the wild ideas.
4. If the results do not meet the problem resolution requirements, the process is repeated on another idea. If no practical ideas emerge, another wild idea is used and the process continues until an acceptable idea is found.

This is an important technique because it produces a surge of ideas that are often highly cost-effective.

Wishful Thinking

Applied properly, this approach can free you from unnecessary but unrecognized assumptions that you are making about the scenario of concern.

Procedure for Use

Generally, the steps to follow in applying the technique are as follows:

1. State the question, goal, situation, or problem.
2. Assume anything is possible.
3. Using fantasy, make statements such as: 'What I really want to

do is . . .' or 'If I could choose any answer to this question, it would be . . .'

4. Examine each fantasy and their statements and, using this as stimulation, return to reality and make statements such as: 'Although I really cannot do that, I can do . . .' or 'It seems impractical to do that, but I believe we can accomplish the same thing by . . .'

5. If necessary, repeat Steps 3 and 4.

Example for Use

1. How can I learn more about how customers use my product?
2. I can be any size or shape I want.
3. I will just step inside one of the products shipped today and peer out at my customer and observe how he or she uses the product.
4. Well, I don't think I can accomplish that feat, but I can get a customer's agreement to let me observe my product under use at their facility and videotape employees at work using my product.

Role Play

Show participants an interesting scene from a movie for inspiration. An automotive parts company working on waging war against waste (WWW) saw a scene from *Rang De Basanti* and then created five skits on different aspects on cost reduction using the list of characters. The participants are asked to step into the shoes of a character. The usual list of characters is hero, heroine, villain, director, comedian and character actor. The subject will be the problem chosen and the group enacts actual situations for a better understanding of the problem.

Idea Generation

It is worth remembering that the rules for thinking are totally different from the rules for doing. You can set up a $100 million factory in your mind, study the mathematical implications and destroy it without losing a single dollar. However, as soon as the first brick is physically laid, or the first employee hired, you start losing money.

Do not analyse your thoughts during idea generation. Remove all boundaries. Apply analysis only in the fourth stage of the creative thinking process. It is ideal to train trainers in the thinking tools and then encourage them to deliver training to the teams.

*

'There is always a well-known solution to every problem—neat, practical and wrong,' said Rags. 'Some ideas are immediately accepted. Because they are old!'

'Okay. Let's start,' I said. 'How to teach Tulu to all the kids?'

'The child should be in an environment where everyone speaks that language and only that language.'

'My nephew spoke beautiful Tulu till he went to school. But at school in Chennai, no one could understand a word he said. The other kids spoke Tamil. The teacher said, "Teach him a language we can understand."'

'That is a challenge. Make him see Tulu movies. Get him to speak to relatives who speak Tulu. Hire help who can speak the language. Most of all make him fall in love with the language, with its age-old proverbs and stories and heritage. Take him back to his hometown on special days to keep in touch with people and events.'

*

Use Checklists to Develop Ideas

Checklists help generate ideas in a systematic way. Once a problem is identified, teams can use checklists to explore all areas and issues that are associated with the problem. They help the team think and are often in the form of questions. Many of the mapping tools, like 6M, are just like checklists, encouraging you to be systematic in your approach.

The simplest tools include checklists like the questions which, why, where, when, how and who. Thinkers from Plato onwards have developed hundreds of thinking tools which are as easy to learn as the three Rs (reading, [w]riting, [a]rithmetic).

The following checklist was created by Alex Osborn, an advertising genius and inventor of the creativity technique called 'Brainstorming'. Apply it to develop ideas on a chosen problem. Teams can then discuss the problem together.

The Checklist:

- Put to other uses? *(Make your nephew write a Tulu play.)*
- Adapt? Is there anything else like this? What does this tell you? Is the past comparable? *(Let him translate English plays into Tulu.)*
- Modify? Give it a new angle? *(Discuss the characters in plays.)*
- Magnify? Can it be duplicated, multiplied or exaggerated?
- Minimize? Can anything be taken away? Made smaller? Lowered?
- Shortened? Lengthened? Omitted? Broken up?
- Substitute? Different ingredients used? Other material?
- Other processes? Other places? Other approaches? Other tone of voice? Someone else?
- Rearrange? Swap components? Alter the pattern, sequence or layout? Change the pace or schedule? Transpose cause and effect?
- Reverse? Opposites? Backwards? Reverse roles?

(How can your community meet to encourage young people in a Tulu quiz? A Tulu magazine using English script, till the ancient Tulu script can be rejuvenated.)

*

'With this love for your culture, however, you need to fight the tendency to become parochial,' said Rags. 'The capacity to love other cultures, learn about them and see the essential humanity of all human beings is the challenge.'

'How can we preserve and promote living cultures?' I asked.

'You can prevent beautiful old homes and temples from falling to ruins...'

'Why don't you give me a checklist?'

'There is the usual 27-points plan...'

'Maybe you can start right away with a short e-bulletin?'

1. Start a Facebook page for your community worldwide.
2. Start a website sharing information and pictures.
3. Create interest in beautiful family homes and provide information on the website.
4. Share dates of temple festivals.
5. Create interest in a calendar of dates for dance programmes, dramas and telling of ancient stories.
6. Create a museum of artifacts. To start with, it can be a gallery on the web.
7. Create an annual event to honour achievers in many fields and provide a feast of local philosophy in the programme.
8. Create a tour of heritage homes and local places of interest. Involve a travel agent in this.
9. Have a worldwide competition of recipes and award prizes; publish a book on the subject.
10. Collect information on all customs and ceremonies from birth to death.
11. Discuss old proverbs and how they can be applied to modern times.

12. Rebuild ruined buildings and temples. This is especially critical in the aftermath of destructive conflicts and natural disasters. Contact UNESCO which has a programme to preserve world heritage sites guided by the Convention for the Protection of World Cultural and National Heritage, so that your grandchildren can see and enjoy their heritage. INTACH too does some of this work.

13. Find historians, encourage writers and universities to record and publish local history.

14. Invite volunteers through UNESCO's cultural heritage wing to mobilize skilled volunteers in archaeology, conservation of monuments and buildings, care of manuscripts, revival of traditional crafts and craft employment, protection of indigenous language and promotion of traditional medicine.

15. Create a book on traditional medicine and encourage practitioners to set up a centre. Encourage families to share their traditional medicines.

'How sad it is to see the heads of statues cut off at Angkor Wat sold to traders in Bangkok by the Pol Pot,' I said pensively 'UNESCO is trying to recreate the old magic But it is but a drop in the ocean of destruction. Why can't the Cambodians be trained and involved more in making their land a magnet for tourists the way Thailand is? Perhaps it is time we sent this checklist to all Indian heritage sites for local people to come up with innovative ideas.'

16. Create a website to sell local arts and crafts. Involve a major retail chain in this.

'Somehow most retail chains in India seem more involved in selling western cosmetics and clothes instead of developing local arts, crafts and textiles. I wish some brilliant local business can see the potential for this. So far one only sees boring government organizations doing this,' I said.

'Government organizations don't have to be boring . . .' said Rags.

17. Hold a poetry and song mela in historical locations.
18. Have summer and holiday courses for children and young people to learn songs, dance and crafts.
19. Encourage major festivals in the cities to invite artistes from six programme areas: dance, music, theatre, publishing, visual arts and media arts.
20. Artistes and writers need to help with skill development in publishing, as gallery curators and theatre company administrators. These interventions should strengthen the capacity of people to know themselves and express themselves to the world.

'I am not sure that unity is possible when we build such diversity,' I said.

'You will be surprised; by encouraging cultural diversity, paradoxically we can help find the common ground for living together in a unified nation,' said Rags.

21. Dialogues for peace and tolerance can be set up where there is civil unrest or war. Communities can help such cooperation. Youth exchange programmes especially during festivals can promote understanding.
22. Preserved objects also validate memories.
23. Tangible culture includes buildings, historic places,

monuments, clothing and other artifacts worth preserving. The disciplines that are required to be focussed on are musicology, archival science, restoration, art conservation, architectural conservation, film preservation, photographic record preservation and digital preservation.

24. Grandfathers and grandmothers should receive employment in storytelling, writing and preserving skills from the past.

25. Heritage walks for kids is a cool new idea in many cities. A 'culture hut' needs to be set up in each community.

26. Intangible culture—social values and traditions, customs and practices, aesthetic and spiritual beliefs, artistic impression, language etc.—needs to be preserved and encouraged.

27. Preservation of natural heritage (encompassing the countryside, flora and fauna—scientifically known as bio-diversity), geological elements (including mineralogical, geomorphologic, paleontological—scientifically known as geo-diversity), ethno-botany (rare breeds conservation, preservation of heirloom plants etc.) are other necessary efforts.

The four professional dimensions of such preservation include:

- Cultural heritage repatriation
- Cultural heritage management
- Cultural property law
- Cultural tourism.

**

'Hey, we need to network the power of young parents and young people to do this,' I said.

'Somehow most of us only think of our own tiny homes to the exclusion of everything else. This results in bonsai human beings,' Rags said.

I thought of war-torn Sri Lanka. I had visited an orphanage outside Colombo. It was just after the evening meal with 3- to 6-year-olds. Suddenly there was the sound of a bomb exploding (or was it just fireworks?). A single child started howling. In seconds, all the 150 kids were crying. It was such a desolate, heart-rending scene. Children were crying and there were no loving mothers to comfort them. The worst tragedy of wars is that the endless chains, the links that carry culture from one generation to the other are thoughtlessly broken.

'During World War II, thousands of kids were orphaned in the bombing of London,' said Rags, reading my thoughts as usual. 'The children were taken to state-run orphanages— fed, clothed and sheltered. But they began to die in alarming numbers. Research showed that they died because no one loved them, cuddled them or spoke to them. They died because they were deprived of the physical warmth of mothers who would have naturally "mothered" them. What we need to worry about is not heart attacks but loneliness attacks.'

I was sad and knew how they must have felt. At least I had my mom for sixteen years.

'Remember,' said Rags, 'besides being a son, a branch manager, a brother or a lover, you are first and foremost a person, one who needs to be acknowledged and affirmed by you.'

We moved on to the next folder.

**

Personal Wellness

Your Personal Well-being Assessment

Answer Yes (Y) / No (N)   Y   N

1. Are your decisions carefully thought out?
2. Have you tried analysing your own potential?
3. Are your goals designed to maximize your potential?
4. Do you brood over the harm caused by people who have hurt you?
5. Do you handle your emotions in a mature way?
6. Do you know anyone that you trust, with whom you can confidently share your emotions?
7. Do you plan 'happiness breaks' every day?
8. Do you generally accept your feelings as being an important part of you?
9. Have you overcome any habits that prevent you from achieving your full potential?
10. Do you love and appreciate yourself?
11. Do you imagine success in all your activities?
12. Do you often consciously erase memories of negative past experiences?
13. Is it easy for you to develop new concepts or ideas?
14. Do you understand new concepts and help implement them?
15. Do you ever try to visualize the outcome of events before they happen?
16. Are you satisfied with your attitude towards work?
17. Is your attitude generally positive?
18. Do you consult others but make your own decisions?
19. Do you carefully select the music, books, movies and websites that you listen to, watch and read?

20. Do you live in a peaceful area where rule of law prevails?
21. Do you provide encouragement and support to people around you?
22. Is it possible for you to determine how others see you?
23. Do you grab opportunities even when people discourage you?
24. Do you admire people who always seem to be winning or achieving?
25. Do you know how to get yourself comfortable in new situations?
26. Do you have good ways of dealing with stress?
27. Have your feelings of stress and tension ever kept you from doing as well as you know you can?
28. Do you enjoy dealing with new people or new situations?
29. Would you be confident leading a new initiative in unfamiliar territory?
30. Do you enjoy hobbies that give you joy?
31. Are you confident that you have done your best in the past?
32. Do you have a clear plan for the future?

```
Score
Good: More than 26 Ys
Adequate: More than 20 Ys
Poor: Less than 20 Ys
```

**

Rags and I discussed the various chivalrous arts of war while we looked at the beautiful centre for archery. Men in graceful Gos practised the ancient art of archery, with beautifully personalized bamboo bows and arrows which can be shot at a target 150 metres away. Set against two large grassy mounds, the archery stadium was set beside beautifully painted old world buildings replete with intricate paintings.

The men broke into a wild dance to applaud every time someone hit the target. Local women in their most colourful garments sang and danced to distract the competitors; small tables held ara for the celebrations on the archery field.

'I used to paint so well, when I was in school,' I said regretfully. 'And I loved playing the guitar.'

'Anything stopping you now? Let us pick up a guitar at the next village,' Rags said, looking at our four-legged friend who was looking at us dolefully, with liquid eyes.

'I think he wants dinner,' I said.

'He's sure got his fundas right,' said Rags.

I showed him some parts of the Kalari technique I had learnt right after Mom died, to deal with my sadness and anger.

Kalari is a martial art from Kerala, where every muscle and sinew is used in combat. The technique is fast and furious. The origin of Kerala's Kalaripayattu dates back to the ninth century. Kalaripayattu includes strikes, kicks, grappling and healing methods. Young boys of seven were taught Kalari in schools. They learnt to dance and turn, twist on the ground and take royal leaps till they became so loose-jointed, loose-limbed and supple as to be almost contrary to nature. Kathakali dancers who knew martial arts were believed to be markedly better than other performers.

Rags had an idea. 'Let's use it as a thinking tool.'

**

Take a verb from the following list and 'check' the item against certain aspects of the problem. The comprehensive list of verbs helps reduce the possibility that a solution might be overlooked.

You sequentially move through the following list of verbs to suggest possible solutions to the problem.

multiply	distort	fluff up	extrude
divide	rotate	bypass	repel
eliminate	flatten	add	protect
subdue	squeeze	subtract	segregate
invert	complement	lighten	integrate
separate	submerge	repeat	symbolize
transpose	freeze	thicken	abstract
unify	soften	stretch	dissect

Example for Use

A common problem in project management is the plan's failure to meet the desired schedule, either at the initiation of the project or during the course of implementing the project.

Approaches to rearrange resources to meet the schedule date for an information systems development project:

Multiply	Increase the number of personnel
	Increase the amount of the project budget
	Increase the tools available
Eliminate	Eliminate some of the functionality of the system
Subdue	Simplify the design
Invert	Design a prototype to test early on instead of at the end
Separate	Separate the critical from non-critical activities
Unify	Combine modules
Distort	Worst-scenario formulation
Rotate	Personnel

Squeeze	Schedule
	Resources
	Requirements
Complement	People skills with computer skills
Submerge	Egos
	Distractions
	Less important problems
Freeze	Specifications
	Personnel (disallow transfers to other projects)

**

'You could also take away cultural heritage, bit by bit, and protect it in a museum,' said Rags, returning to our earlier topic.

'Like the British so generously took away everything to the British Museum,' I said wryly.

'Well, I don't see you doing much about the heritage you still have left in plenty. The other day I saw a beautiful temple tank in Chennai being used as a garbage dump, so that some builder could put a multistorey building on it. And do you know the Palar, which fed the ancient Tamil civilizations, has been leached dry because all the tanks feeding it have been "reclaimed" to build luxury apartments? Sand on its bed has been plundered in lorry-loads in the dead of night.'

'Do you want me to do something to the sand mafia and get killed?' I asked.

'No. But you can stop buying sand for building your factories from them,' said Rags. 'The Native American tradition has a custom, where a tribal elder is required to represent the interests of the seventh generation in the future. The tribal council has to consider how its decision will affect the future seventh generation. We need to apply this benchmark for all important decisions we are taking today.'

He introduced me next to Attribute Matching.

**

Attribute Matching

Attribute matching is a simple method which breaks down the stereotypes which are very common among many of us.

Procedure for Use

1. Come up with a procedure or process that is totally different from the process or product to be improved.
2. List attributes of the new product or process.
3. Apply each attribute to the product or process being considered and arrive at alternative solutions.

Example for Use

Let us say that we want to design a method of work which is as interesting as a holiday. You would then list out the attributes of a holiday as follows:

A holiday is a time when one can go away on picnics and play games and listen to music

A holiday is when you enjoy and meet new people

A holiday is when you enjoy leisure time activities and different sports like canoeing and water skiing

A holiday is when you catch up on your reading

A holiday is when you spend more time with your family

Now, in attribute matching, you apply each of the attributes to the work situation. For example, you say, I would like my work to involve spending more time with my family. This can lead to the idea that families can be invited to the workplace or helped to take up jobs in your workplace. Family get-togethers every month will also provide opportunities when family members are involved in contributing to the individual company as in telemarketing or with summer jobs for the kids. Both ideas are being implemented in many corporations. You can use the holiday ideas to create daily happiness breaks at work: a reading break, a chess break, a laugher break.

You can use any word as a key to enter the domain of a problem in attribute matching. This enables you to study a problem by importing ideas from a totally different field.

**

'See the burrs which are sticking on your pants,' said Rags. 'Poor Sirius probably has some stuck on his paws.'

Sure enough, Sirius put out his paw to me as we settled down for dinner. 'The idea for Velcro came from this,' said Rags.

There were burrs, which I pulled out with the tweezers from Rags's manicure kit. I had a good laugh about the manicure kit.

'Well, this is the age of the metrosexual. You know everyone loves Beckham,' he said.

'Did you hear about the trisexual? As in homosexual, bisexual?'

'No, what is trisexual?' he asked.

'It is Try Anything Once!' I laughed.

He gave me the 'what an idiot' look and walked off to look at the stars, with Sirius close on his heels. The dog was such a fool. I did everything for him, fed him, cleaned him, played with him, even removed burrs from his paw.

But he just adored Rags, who did nothing but pet him. But that, I guessed, was the nature of love. Those who needed it the least (and in my opinion deserved it the least), got the most of it.

I was all alone in the silence of the night. Suddenly I wanted to reach out to Rima.

> **Sirius says Hi! to Coco**

Pat came the reply:

> **GO TO HELL!**

What had I done wrong? Girls were impossible to understand.

> **WHY HVNT U GOT IN TOUCH 4 A WK??**

The phone was fuming in my hands and it sputtered into blankness.

Why couldn't she understand that nothing worked out here as she imagined? Here I was collecting all my courage to say 'I love you', for my first serious love letter. Here I was thinking about her all the time . . . and she didn't even know.

'Why so glum? Is it her?' asked Rags as he ran up to me with a panting Sirius. I gave him a tough look and turned in for the night.

'Never sleep over a quarrel without saying sorry,' whispered Rags as I lay in silence looking at the frosty stars.

Next morning, he handed over a cuddly teddy bear. The zip on its tummy opened to reveal the next questionnaire.

**

Family Bonding

Your Family Health Assessment
Answer Yes (Y) / No (N)   Y   N

1. Is your family important to you?
2. Do you spend quality time with members of your family?
3. Would you like to increase the amount of quality time you spend with your family?
4. Does your family include those outside the nuclear family?
5. Is your family linked together through the Internet, letters or phone calls?
6. Is respect from your family important to you?
7. Do you show appreciation for things your family has done for you?
8. Do you seek to make your family life different from what it is today?
9. Do you do things to bring about a happier marriage and family life?
10. Do you seek out books and classes that would help you to be a successful parent?
11. Do you avoid alcohol and tobacco?
12. Do you speak up adequately in your family?
13. Do you avoid too much fighting in your family?
14. Does your family do fun things together?
15. Are you considerate in handling of misunderstandings between family members?

16. Do you come from a happy family?

17. Do you take steps to strengthen your own character or family ties?

18. Could you possibly use outside help such as counsellors and friends to assist you in attaining a solid family now or in the future?

> Score
> Good: More than 10 Ys
> Adequate: More than 6 Ys
> Poor: Less than 5 Ys

**

'What family?' I asked bleakly. 'My parents are dead.'

Rags looked at me with complete affection and pushed Sirius over to me. Sirius did what he did best. He licked me and leapt all over me with loving whimpers and yelps, nudging me with his paws. He then lay at my feet and looked adoringly at me.

'And then, what about the family you will start with Rima? And all the memories of your parents who loved you and who loved each other so much?'

I felt better.

'The family is the giant shock absorber of society to which the bruised and battered individual returns after doing battle with the world,' said Rags.

'Toffer,' I said.

'Yes. Let's have your take on it.'

'I don't know if modern women can provide that shock absorber. Most of them have careers and are just not interested in being like my mom was.'

'Hey, why can't both partners be shock absorbers? Why can't we all network with our extended families?' said Rags.

'Cities are so impersonal . . . and how can working parents bring up kids properly?'

'It needs a village to bring up a child. Why can't you turn your community into a village? Why can't you build your village in your apartment block or your street?'

I looked at him sternly. Then I couldn't help grinning at him and his endless enthusiasm.

'When I shut the door in the evening and morning, I don't know who lives on either side of me. I don't even know my neighbours,' I said.

'Whose fault is that?' asked Rags.

I thought deeply about my future family, about our home, about everything that Rima could make possible.

But we were not even talking.

'In Bhutan a new constitution gives equal rights to men and women,' said Rags. 'In the past the elders said "a man is nine times better than a woman". I don't know if it's a sign of progress, but they now have a Miss Bhutan in the Miss Universe contest. Young women are starving themselves to achieve the size zero look. Many young women feel fat and ugly. How sad that fashion should dictate a body shape that is unhealthy and impractical . . .'

'Wait till you see Vidya Balan in *The Dirty Picture*,' I said. 'Vidya Balan, in a TV interview said, I don't want to look like a boy! I feel attractive as I am.'

'Good for her!' said Rags.

He told me that the Bhutan Multiple Indicator Survey of 2010 said 68.4 per cent of women felt that their husband has a right to hit or beat them; 54.5 per cent said men can use force when mothers neglect their children; 25 per cent believed that their husbands could beat them if they refused to have sex or burnt the food. This was more among women in small towns and villages, of course.

I could imagine how Rima would react to this. She was the warrior princess type, like my mom.

There are three things it is impossible for a son to save his mother from: sickness, growing old and death—I had read this in a book about the Buddha. How true. Not all my love, my tears, my prayers or my desperate clinging could save my mother.

seven

The next sheaf of papers was titled 'Good Governance'.

*

Good Governance

'Governments in the next ten years should be judged and measured by how happy everyone is,' says David Halpern, adviser to the British prime minister.

The concept of 'good governance' often emerges as a model to compare ineffective economies or political bodies with viable ones. According to the UN, good governance has eight characteristics:

- Participatory
- Following the rule of law
- Effective and efficient
- Accountable
- Transparent
- Responsive
- Equitable
- Inclusive

Good governance defines a consensus-oriented ideal which is difficult to achieve in full. Major donors and international financial institutions like the International Monetary Fund (IMF)

149

or the World Bank are basing their aid and loans on the condition that the recipients undertake reforms ensuring good governance. This is mostly due to the close link between poor governance and corruption. Most of the money meant for development goes into private pockets in a corrupt system.

Emerging concerns of society—democracy, human rights, rights of children and women, women's contribution to economic growth and happiness—must be part of an agenda for good governance. Since concepts such as civil society, decentralization, peaceful conflict management and accountability are often used when defining the concept of good governance, the definition promotes many ideas that closely align with effective democratic governance. President Obama said, 'What Africa needs is not more strong men, it needs stronger democratic institutions that will stand the test of time. Without good governance, no amount of oil or no amount of aid, no amount of effort can guarantee Nigeria's success. But with good governance, nothing can stop Nigeria. We believe that delivering on roads and on electricity and on education will demonstrate the kind of concrete progress that the people of Nigeria are waiting for.'

An aged activist in India, dragged to jail for fighting corruption, says, 'Bring back the black money. Do you know what will happen if Rs 1456 lakh crores come back to India? India will financially be the number one financial power it deserves to be.'

Indeed—each district would get Rs 6000 crores and each village would get Rs 100 crores. No one would need to pay income tax for the next twenty years. Petrol would be priced at Rs 25 a litre, diesel at Rs 15, and milk at Rs 8. There would be no need to pay electricity bills. India's borders would be stronger then the Great Wall of China. Over 1500 universities like Oxford could be opened in India. 28,000 km of rubber roads could be made. Over 2000 hospitals could be built to provide free treatment. Nearly 45 crore people would own their own homes.

An old man went to prison for asking for this, to make India a great nation!

**

'The problem with embedded corruption is that it keeps poor countries poor and poor people starving,' says Rags sombrely.

'What can we do?' I asked him, horrified by the size of the problem.

'The money flowing into private pockets should be rechannelled to give priority to the poor, help women, sustain the environment and create opportunities for livelihood and employment of all types,' he said gravely.

'Occupy Wall Street (OWS) is electrifying New York,' I reflected. 'Thousands of young people are protesting about the way they have been taken for a ride by the greedy 1per cent fat cats who control the economy. "We are the 99 per cent" is the OWS slogan. This is based on the fact that 1per cent of the world's population owns 99 per cent of its resources. A young law student at the corner of Broadway and Wall Street shouted at the police protecting a bank: "I am not moving. This is the bank that took away my parents' house. You can arrest me but I am not moving!" People are fed up of being pawns. A thirty-year-old transporter in Delhi slapped a minister in a public meeting recently for being corrupt . . .'

'This type of corruption hits at every child in the womb,' said Rags. 'Do you know 250 million families live on the brink of poverty in India? Which means pregnant mothers, who eat last in a home, do not get the micronutrients necessary for the child's brain, blood and bones to grow normally.'

Is our country producing human beings who will never be equal, physically or mentally, to others, I wondered.

'The mother's hunger stretches out its spectral finger into the innocent life of a schoolboy who is not able to comprehend his lessons. Or the young girl with tuberculosis, coughing her lungs out into a bloody towel. It is the food and dignity of these helpless citizens that is pouring into protected foreign accounts. So what the government needs to do is to protect the life opportunities of future generations and the natural systems on which life depends,' said Rags.

The drive back to Paro by jeep was comfortable. We visited the seat of local government in Paro, Rinchen Pung Dzong, which means 'the fortress built on a heap of jewels'. It is an imposing structure, beautifully painted and decorated. From the large central courtyard rises a five-storey building to the huge basement for the use of the monks; it is truly imposing. The administrative offices line the courtyard.

The annual festival, the Paro Tsechu, held in March or April starts in the courtyard and then shifts to a open space outside. The Tibetans feel that it is necessary to pray for the long life of all humans, trees, animals, birds and water.

The central courtyard is the academy for monks to study. A beautiful painting of a parable decorates the lobby of the Dzong, where the government operates and the monks reside and lend their wisdom. This is a good combination where good governance is supported by religious values and ethics.

Respect for team work is extolled in a painting where four creatures help grow a tree:

A bird plants the seed
The rabbit waters it
The monkey guards it
And an elephant helps them gather the fruits.

All should be respected. The small bird is the seniormost, says our guide.

The gods of the four directions are honoured. The kala chakra shows the punishments meted out by divine force to those who do wrong.

It is an excellent visual communication attempt.

I went back to the sheaf of papers.

**

The UNDP Human Development Report says, 'What we need to work for is an enabling environment in which all can enjoy long, healthy and creative lives.'

The five aspects of sustainable human development are:

- Empowerment
- Cooperation
- Equity
- Sustainability
- Security

The UNDP focuses on four critical elements of sustainable human development:

1. Eliminating poverty
2. Creating jobs and sustainable livelihoods
3. Protecting and regenerating the environment.
4. Promoting the advancement of women.

**

'The British sucked the wealth and heritage and confidence of the country and took them away to England. Today our Indian "leaders" are sucking away our very life blood and stockpiling it in Swiss banks. Corruption is sucking away the life and vitality of the country,' said Rags.

'At the village level, gram sabhas should discuss everything about the village, specially spending of grants. People should get together and punish corrupt officials. In Bhutan, there are 205 gewogs or local administrative units. The heads of each help solve disputes. The final authority is the king, whose word is final,' I said.

'"An invasion of armies can be resisted, but not an idea whose time has come", said Victor Hugo. The time has come to end corruption,' said Rags.

'Let us create high-performing teams, working to build a great nation, in every part of our country.'

High performing groups	Low performing groups
Informal	Rank is right
Experimental	Little risk taking
Action-oriented	Formal relationships
High cooperation	Privileges and perks
Low defensiveness	Many status symbols
High levels of trust	Rules rigidly enforced
Little second-guessing	Slow action/great care
Few trappings of power	Much protective paperwork
High respect for learning	Decision-making done at top

Few rules and high flexibility	High levels of fear and anxiety
Low levels of anxiety and fear	Your problem is yours, not ours
Empowering of team members	Well-defined chain of command
Little discounting or disparaging	Learning limited to formal training
Failures seen as problems to solve	Many information-giving meetings
Decisions made at the action point	Trouble puts people on the defensive
People easily cross organizational lines	Little problem-solving below top level
Many informal problem-solving meetings	Crossing organizational lines forbidden
People pick up and correct the errors of others	Need to bury mistakes or whitewash them
Trouble puts people into 'problem-solving' mode	Carefully formulated rules and regulations
Willingness to take risks and learn from mistakes	Complaints and discomforts go underground

'Why can't the government listen to citizens?' I asked.

'Honest criticism is always hard to take, particularly from a relative, a friend, an acquaintances or a stranger!' said Rags.

We both laughed and went back to some serious

sightseeing. We visited the National Museum in Paro. High on a hill, it has fabulous views. The circular original building was damaged by an earthquake and has been shut down. The museum has been shifted to another building.

'Anyone can look for fashion in a boutique or history in a museum. The creative explorer looks for history in a hardware store and fashion in an airport,' said Rags, quoting Robert Wieder.

Beautiful masks are preserved in the museum. The masked dances were meant to communicate dharmic messages or to purify the space. The stag and hound dance tells of how a stag, being hunted by a hunter and his hounds, took refuge in a cave with a sage, Milarepa. The sage talked to the hunter and asked him if he knew when he himself would die. He made the hunter feel compassion for the hunted. There are dances by the four skeletons which help viewers to come to terms with death and the cemetery.

We sat down to look at an exciting tool.

*

Tent Thinking vs Marble Palace Thinking

A bank wanted to rapidly open branches at a minimal cost. They were not sure which locations were most likely to succeed. An innovation laboratory came up with the idea of using existing organizations such as schools, petrol bunks and panchayat halls to set up branches. This solution had two advantages:

1. It was inexpensive
2. It could be easily dismantled or closed if not successful

Today, the speed at which corporations are required to grow involves experiments. An experiment should be inexpensive. In fact, in an experiment, there is no success or failure; there is only feedback.

This, essentially, is Tent Thinking. A tent can be put up, change shape; it can be expanded or reduced and it can be dismantled and put up elsewhere.

Marble Palace Thinking involves a fascination with permanence. Permanent structures, people and systems are expensive and difficult to dismantle. Permanent staff is a fixed overhead which cannot be reduced as a swift response to falling demand in a recessionary market. This is the Marble Palace mentality.

Success in today's scenario goes to those who are swift, dynamic and able to respond to mercurial changes in the environment. Adaptability is the most important quality this millennium demands. Marble palaces become fixed overheads, which are difficult to adapt to any other use.

Analogies

The use of analogies, like metaphors, can be a valuable tool in stimulating creativity, both in problem definition and problem solving. Einstein often used this technique as a way to visualize and solve problems. The development of the analogies/metaphors creativity technique is generally credited to Edward de Bono. However, Aristotle spoke of the value of metaphor almost 2200 years ago: 'Now strange words simply puzzle us; ordinary words convey only what we know already; it is from metaphor that we can best find something fresh.'

An analogy is a similarity between two things that may not be immediately evident. By the use of analogies, an individual or group can often find a new insight and approach to the nature of a problem and thus its resolution.

Procedure for Use

Often, one can force analogies, for example, 'How is this problem like a time bomb?' to examine and restructure a query. To use the technique of applying analogies:

1. Identify the essence of the query that you are facing, for example, the query might be: 'How can we improve the way we work with other departments?' Key to the statement is the goal of 'improving'.
2. Create a list of devices and methods that are particularly relevant to the key concept—improving. For example, runners follow a training regimen to improve, which includes a combination of factors: diet, exercise and psychological techniques.
3. Review your specific question in the context of each device or method on your list.
4. All potentially positive features of the ideas are identified and the deficiencies are used to give the direction for improvement, preserving the element of novelty while the idea is modified to make it feasible.

Free Fall

The capacity to let go is rare as most humans seek security. But to stand still is to risk even more—it is to risk being overtaken by change. It is to risk being 'dragged, an unwilling victim to be sacrificed on the altar of technology,' as Jawaharlal Nehru feared.

Free fall is like bungee jumping. You let go without knowing definitely what will happen. Creative ideas are a kind of free fall. You generate ideas that have never been suggested or heard before. You risk the contempt of your peers, their jeers and laughter.

There is the old story of Columbus, who discovered America. When he returned his friends said, 'Anyone could have done it. You just kept sailing west till you found America. We too could have done it.' Columbus brought out an egg and said, 'Make it stand up straight.' No one could do it. They said 'It can't be done.' Columbus tapped the egg lightly on the table, so that it cracked slightly to form a stable surface and then made it stand. Everyone said, 'That is cheating. You can't break the egg.' Columbus said, 'Who said you can't break the egg? You are imagining limitations and boundaries that are not there. Then you are saying it can't be done. That is why you could not have discovered America.'

**

Rags gave me a little pink slip, neatly typed.

'The horse is here today, but the automobile is only a novelty—a fad'—President of Michigan Savings Bank, advising against investing in the Ford Motor Company

---

I remembered a trip I took to Jharia, a coal mining town near Dhanbad in Bihar. Coal mining has created a subterranean world full of methane gas, just below the surface of the earth. As I walked through the bare, fire-burnt earth, suddenly I almost stepped on a patch of fiery embers. My companion grabbed my arm and pulled me back. 'If you had stepped on that, you would have fallen through into a fiery inferno,' he said. He also explained how, for those living in this smoky, fiery place, your house may suddenly fall into the pit during the night, never to be found again.

'How do people live here?' I asked.

'They got used to it,' he said.

Many suffered from respiratory diseases. They usually sent their kids away as far away as possible. Those who had no choice, just lived there.

Reading my thoughts, Rags spoke of people who lived in places that were submerged every day, during high tide, by the sea. 'They just take their bundles and babies and run, only to return during low tide!' he said.

'And what about displaced people, who are refugees, displaced by wars? Reconciliation for post-crisis and disintegrating societies? The fact that you have a normal life is quite abnormal,' he continued.

I went back to the sheaf of papers.

**

Good governance is participatory, transparent and accountable. It provides a safe, stable environment for people to live and work in. Political, social and economic actions are undertaken to help the poorest and the most vulnerable.

Besides government, private sector and civil society can also contribute to these goals.

According to the Corruption Perceptions Index (CPI) released by Transparency International (TI) in 2011, India fares rather poorly in this area. Where a score of 10 is the least corrupt—

India and its neighbours

Rank	Country	Score
75	China	3.6
86	Sri Lanka	3.3
95	India	3.1
120	Bangladesh	2.7
134	Pakistan	2.5

Cleanest countries

Rank	Country	Score
1	New Zealand	9.5
2	Denmark	9.4
3	Finland	9.4
4	Sweden	9.3
5	Singapore	9.2

Most corrupt countries

Rank	Country	Score
182	Somalia	1.0
182	N Korea	1.0
180	Myanmar	1.5
180	Afghanistan	1.5
177	Uzbekistan	1.6
	Turkmenistan	
	Sudan	

CPI focuses on corruption in the public sector, involving public officials, civil servants or politicians. The data sources used to compile the index include questions relating to the abuse of power and bribery of public officials, kickbacks in public procurement, embezzlement of public funds and such. In that sense, CPI covers both the administrative and political aspects of corruption. Huguette Labelle, chairperson of Transparency International, says that when it comes to combating corruption, India is definitely moving in the right direction, despite its disappointing showing in the recent survey.

The surveys created an incentive for people to do something about corruption. With governments, Transparency International has developed a number of 'integrity pacts' to be used during bidding to ensure full transparency between bidders and the entity seeking the bid. If anyone is caught cheating, they're disqualified or have to pay a fine. The idea is to try and get companies to band together in a zero tolerance mode, no matter what the sector.

**

'Good governance is everyone's responsibility!' I said. Rags applauded enthusiastically. And Sirius licked me all over in appreciation.

eight

In India the concept of wealth has always meant much more than money. The Ashta Lakshmis (the eight Lakshmis) point to wealth in many other tangible and intangible forms: 'wealth' in the context of the Ashta Lakshmis means prosperity, good health, knowledge, strength, progeny and power. The Ashta Lakshmis are always depicted and worshipped in a group in temples. They comprise:

- **Adi Lakshmi:** the primeval Lakshmi or Maha Lakshmi, an ancient form of Lakshmi as daughter of the sage Bhrigu.
- **Dhana Lakshmi:** the goddess of money and gold.
- **Dhanya Lakshmi:** the goddess of grain, the giver of agricultural wealth.
- **Gaja Lakshmi:** the giver of animal wealth like cattle and elephants. Swami Chidananda interprets Gaja Lakshmi as the giver of the power of royalty. According to Hindu mythology, Gaja Lakshmi brought back the wealth lost by Indra (the king of the gods) from the ocean.
- **Santana Lakshmi:** the bestower of offspring.
- **Veera Lakshmi** or **Dhairya Lakshmi:** the bestower of valour in battles and courage and strength for overcoming difficulties in life.

- **Vijaya Lakshmi** or **Jaya Lakshmi:** the giver of victory, not only in battles but also in conquering hurdles in order to beget success.
- **Vidya Lakshmi:** the bestower of the knowledge of arts and sciences.

'Money spent on experiences make people happier than buying things. The feeling of well-being comes from being connected and loved by friends and the community,' said Rags.

Was there a way to achieve reasonable economic growth without destroying the environment, I wondered. Was it possible to amass great wealth while enjoying the boons of the Ashta Lakshmis?

Economic growth is an increase in the value of goods and services that a country produces and sells, compared to the previous year. 'Imagine a man selling all the machines in his factory and saying that he made a profit. Often, economic growth is measured this way, ignoring the loss of natural, social and cultural capital,' said Rags.

'The standard of living has increased dramatically in many countries but happiness has remained static or even decreased,' he continued.

'Do happy people live longer than those who are depressed?' I asked.

'The difference in life spans seems to be about nine years,' said Rags. 'Heavy cigarette smoking can knock off six years of your life,' he added slyly.

'I don't smoke that much,' I said defensively.

'This is like being slightly pregnant,' countered Rags, the smart alec as always.

'I remember reading Nobel Laureate Simon Kuznets. He

said that GDP can never be a measure of economic prosperity or the nation's welfare. To measure how a country is doing you have to ask *what* is growing, not just how much it is growing. After all anything can make the economy grow: more sickness, more crime, pollution, natural disasters, war, resource depletion. So long as we are spending money the economy will grow,' I said grandly.

'Think about it, it's really strange,' I continued. 'The more trees we cut down, the more the economy will grow, because GDP counts only what we extract. It does not measure the impact of the destroyed forest. The more minerals we extract from the earth, more the economy will grow, because we are not measuring the impact of the devastation we wreak on the earth. Devastation that will impact unborn generations, when the water from our rivers is too polluted to drink, and plastic bottles of water grow the economy.'

'The critical thing is, even when there is economic growth, a majority of the people can still be poor and hungry. This happens when all the wealth is in the hands of a few and the majority is poor. Sometimes this wealth is created by selling goods that are harmful to mankind. Like selling drugs,' said Rags.

'Even then, the wealth earned out of the misery of others is still not distributed, but kept safely in the hands of a few,' I reflected.

'Sometimes there is economic development generated by creating goods of higher value, like the handbags created in Vaniyambadi in Tamil Nadu and sold on the catwalks of Paris. Or textiles woven in the unsanitary bylanes of Benares and sold in New York at many times the price,' said Rags.

'It would be good if some of this money went to those weaving, or working in leather or embroidering. It does not,' I agreed.

'The business cycle is made of booms and busts that occur over a period of years,' I continued. 'What happens is overproduction of goods resulting in large inventories that cannot be sold, overexpansion of credit followed by piling up of debt. This inhibits purchasing. Do you recall the 2002 boom and the bust of 2008–09?'

'The Green Revolution of the 1960s introduced grain hybrids and increased yields. This spurred population growth, but the standard of living remained stagnant.' Rags had the facts on his fingertips. 'There is a synergy between the rise of art and economic growth. The ancient emperors provided the support needed for poets, builders, musicians and dancers. The Bavarian monarchy wanted the area to be not merely a centre of industry but also the world capital of music. Art has no immediate commercial value. But the attitude that creates great art—the internal search for excellence, the stretching out towards innovation—are also the ingredients of sustained economic progress.'

Rags's thoughts were always like stones thrown into the silent pool of my mind. They challenged and stimulated me.

'How great it would be if every company had a chief happiness officer (CHO). And what prevents every city and town or country from having a CHO?' I suggested.

Rags was thrilled by my suggestion. 'Economic growth and happiness are not synonymous,' he said. 'Our greed for money and greed for power are destroying the very essence of the human being; this wanton greed is responsible for the destruction of Mother Earth's ecosystem which sustains the very life on this planet. We can cushion ourselves and our Happiness Quotient against booms and busts by having wonderful families and friends. Research shows that friendship and love can ward off germs, just like stress can cause illness.'

I read aloud from the paper:

We need to ponder on the unforgivable deaths of hundreds of millions of lives through war, civil strife, acts of terrorism, starvation and malnutrition, lack of basic healthcare services and other manmade calamities. Bhutan has borne the brunt of flash floods, landslides, windstorms, fires and earthquakes. Sadly South Asia is home to 41 per cent of the world's poor people.

'Much will depend on what use we make of the vast opportunities offered by the market economy, democratic politics, an independent media, social arrangement for equity and public provisions of human security,' says Amartya Sen.

**

'I read somewhere about the Lipstick Index; the sale of cosmetics shoots up when times are bad,' I said.

'Religion, spirituality and philosophy also become popular during hard times,' said Rags. 'Surprisingly, tough times and negative life experiences actually improve the level of life satisfaction and happiness. People feel a sense of mastering when they overcome negative experiences. To struggle and overcome is good and produces a sense of control over one's life.'

We looked at the next exercise together.

**

Boundary Examination Technique

The objective of this technique is to restructure assumptions (boundaries to our thinking) and provide new ways of looking at the problem. Another way of thinking about a situation is to try to suspend assumptions. Senge says that 'suspending assumptions is a lot like seeing leaps of abstraction and inquiring into the reasoning behind the abstraction'. Boundary expansion is used primarily to question various frames of reference in defining a problem. Boundary examinations are based upon the assumption that a problem's boundaries are neither correct nor incorrect. The objective is to restructure the assumption of a problem to provide a new way for looking at it.

The major strengths of the technique are its potential for

1) Producing more provocative problem definitions
2) Clarifying often indistinguishable problem boundaries
3) Demonstrating the importance of formulating flexible problem definitions
4) Coping with management teams that are overly precise in their problem definitions.

Procedure for Use

1. Describe the problem as presently understood.
2. Identify key elements of the definition and examine them to reveal underlying assumptions.
3. Analyse each assumption to determine its causes and effects.

4. Restate the problem based on your deeper understanding of the elements of the problem.

**

Rags and I settled down to discuss an exercise for social bonding.

**

Social Bonding

Your Social Health Assessment
Answer Yes (Y) / No (N)   Y   N

1. Do I try to create a positive field around me, at home, at work, in social situations?
2. Am I friendly to all people—friends and strangers?
3. Am I sincere in what I say and do?
4. Do I ever talk destructively behind people's backs?
5. Could I possibly pay more attention to others' needs?
6. Do I receive help and support from friends?
7. Am I able to act independently?
8. Is shaking hands or remembering names important to me?
9. Do I like meeting new people?
10. Do I avoid being too loud, boisterous and talkative in the wrong situations?
11. Am I confident in most situations?
12. Can I easily carry on a conversation with others in many different areas of interest?
13. Do I say what I believe in?
14. Do I keep promises?

15. Do I concern myself with world challenges or problems? Do I keep in touch with current events?
16. In certain social situations, do I ever give verbal support to ethical or moral standards that are different from what I personally believe in?
17. Are there any community organizations that I would benefit from joining?
18. Do I stay away from toxic organizations?
19. Do I get along with people I disagree with?
20. Am I able to deal with conflict constructively?

Score
Good: 10 or more Ys
Adequate: 6 or more Ys
Poor: Less than 5 Ys

Bring Veer Rasa into the Organization

Turning ordinary men into matchless warriors full of the enthusiasm to win can definitely improve performance. Gandhiji did just that, using his magic two-word mantras to infuse courage into the freedom struggle: 'Do or Die', 'Quit India', 'Vande Mataram'.

Among the nava rasas, courage is key to the life of a warrior: a corporate warrior is no different and needs real courage. Wonder is developed from courage. The rapture of courage is produced by means of energy, perseverance, optimism, presence of mind and kindness. Courage and bravery are definitely feel-good emotions. Courage is represented on the stage by firmness, patience, heroism, pride, zeal, valour and wit. Bravery fills you with enthusiasm, energy and spontaneity. Bravery is not just bravery in war.

It is the small, everyday acts of courage that each of us is called upon to manifest in the face of obstacles. The ability to sacrifice, which is the core of emotional intelligence, is a part of Veer Rasa. The ability to persist in the face of difficulties is a part of this. To meet the jealousy and pettiness of the world with gentleness, humour and fearlessness is what it is about. Brilliance and elegance belong to the true warrior who aligns himself with the powerful forces of goodness. 'Josh', wakefulness, energy and boundless enthusiasm are an expression of this energy.

Action plan to bring courage and Veer Rasa into your life

* Enjoy the thrill of overcoming obstacles.
* Do not be cast down by failure; instead enjoy the excitement of solving the problem.
* Be involved in finding solutions to community problems.
* Get involved in speaking up against injustice and resisting evil.

'Always think of alternative solutions to every problem,' Rags reminded me.

**

Alternative Explanations

A young man is pouring a can of beer into the gasoline tank of his car.

Explain rationally: what is this supposed to mean?

Creativity is the generation of alternatives. Any number of explanations are possible.

For instance, the car may have stopped. The beer can may have been the only receptacle the man could find to collect gasoline. Or it could be a new type of experimental car which can run on water or beer.

Ask the team to generate alternative solutions to a large number of problems. Give them a certain number of alternatives to be suggested. For example, 'Do not stop till you have fifty solutions.' Usually, insisting on a certain number of alternatives results in getting that number.

We are willing to jump to conclusions about something confusing that we see. This possibly stems from the primitive need to see danger very early. For early man, survival probably depended on quickly jumping to conclusions—they needed to react before they could think. Today, we need to unlearn this facility and train ourselves out of jumping to conclusions to help our understanding of different situations.

Set your teams to practise generating alternative solutions on a regular basis. This will improve their capacity to become fluent in the generation of ideas.

Devil's Advocate

Play Devil's Advocate. As a discipline, think of the exact opposite of the view you have been holding. If you've been saying 'Yes', get the motivation to say 'No'.

For example, if you are an optimist, work out the motivations of the pessimist. Most of us tend to see situations through the flawed windows of our own nature. We are optimistic or pessimistic and do not really participate with others in understanding all aspects and connotations of a problem. Using the Devil's Advocate approach can help us study all aspects of a problem.

Each of us can walk in the shoes of the adversary. Don't forget, while thinking you should remove all barriers and obstacles. Thinking is the easiest way of testing a solution by exploring all possibilities and prevents any major financial distress. But most people are as careful and timid with their thinking as they are with their actions, and lose the possibility of nurturing creative ideas.

Whilst people feel busy and productive leaping into activity, you can happily be busy doing work which may be non-productive. Thinking should be the major activity of managers.

Creativity helps us to find alternative solutions and progress lies in constantly striving, through innovation, to delight the customer.

**

'Imagine that a nuclear plant providing employment for 3000 people is being installed on the outskirts of your village. Now write a letter to the government why this plant should not be built adjoining your rice fields,' said Rags.

'This is easy,' I said. 'With the radioactive accident happening in Japan, it's on everyone's mind. The nuclear plant could endanger the life and health of seven future generations. In fact right now the whole village is up in arms about the sewage treatment plant being built right through the fields to discharge all that stinking waste into our beautiful river Netravathi.'

'How interesting it would be if a fish in that river could play Devil's Advocate,' said Rags ruminatively.

'You should be shocked that they are trying to change the course of the river goddess Netravathi, to take water to a dry, desert area like Bellary,' I remonstrated. 'Have they no idea how they might create earthquakes by tampering with the course of mighty rivers?'

'They may not be alive to see it. Besides, the mining dons are powerful people and some government officials would have had a lot of money paid into their bank accounts. After all, they too have to get their daughters married!' Rags joked.

'Okay,' he said with a glint in his eye. 'What are you doing about it?'

'Nothing,' I said sheepishly.

'Innovation is good for you. Doing things for others is good for you,' said Rags sternly. 'Accelerating thoughts that happen during the use of thinking tools trigger the brain's novelty-loving reward system. A new creative idea gives you an inexpensive jolt of bliss like a shot of dopamine. So teach the thinking tools to others, even a brief period of a lightened mood can lead to an upward spiral.'

'How?' I asked.

'Write a book,' he said. 'Thinking fast makes people feel excited and elevated. Solving problems makes them feel energetic and powerful. So teach the tools, spread the tools. Go out and change the world.'

How could I fail to be ignited by his burning resolve, his boundless optimism, his endless enthusiasm?

'It is infectious to make innovations and happiness viral,' I said excitedly. 'It is easier than spreading gloom and doom!'

'Well, go back and do something. Every tool I give you, every idea, is for you to share with your friends. Every one of them is a seed that can grow into a mighty tree and transform the earth. When you open your e-mail account you will find everything we have spoken about there. Test it. Practise it. If it is true, share it to create a better world.'

'Woof,' said Sirius reproachfully, bored with all the talk. We walked off to bathe in the pure, pristine stream trickling down the mountain. Sirius loved the water.

I reflected on how much Sirius had changed me. My body was clad in the controlled movements of urban civilization, my eyes guarded and cautious. The dog showed me what it means to lose control, to enjoy the physical, heart-thudding freedom of running and swimming. To jump up to pluck a fruit and to be wild and spontaneous enough to give and receive hugs. To be impulsive and enjoy the Oh! of things. I had become far more fun, bursting often into uninhibited laughter. My face was painted with the myriad emotions that passed through my mind like the colours on a Chinese lantern. I had lost my cool, urban mask, that polite robotic self that had become my everyday self. I was no longer involved in 'impression management'. And it was Sirius who had showed me how.

We looked at the stone houses: unpainted, so elemental and beautiful. Rags passed me a pink slip.

'I roamed the countryside searching for the answers to things I did not understand. Why shells existed on the tops of mountains along with the imprints of coral and plants and seaweed usually found in the sea. Why the thunder lasts a longer time than that which causes it and why immediately on its creation the lightning becomes visible to the eye while thunder requires time to travel. How the various circles of water form around the spot which has been struck by a stone and why a bird sustains itself in the air. These questions and other strange phenomena engaged my thought throughout my life.'—Leonardo da Vinci

'Always retain your curiosity. Sirius will show you how, from minute to minute,' said Rags.

**

Simplify

The whole world is moving towards a simpler way of life that is good for mankind. Start a movement to make people conscious of their carbon footprint. Hold up the motto of the green movement.

- Reduce
- Re-use
- Replace
- Repair

Many clients say 'Refuse' to accept environmentally unsafe practices. Simplicity was the goal of Indian rishis. Opulence and waste are frowned on in a land where N. R. Narayana Murthy of Infosys travels economy class, where the Wipro heir says, 'I am not Mr Premji, I am Rishad!' 'Simplify' is the theme that will help India to make a mark during the downturn. It will be easier in India where scarcity makes 'Simplify' a necessity. Deccan Air had cut the frills out of flying and their slogan was 'Simplifly'. Today, aristocratic Kingfisher Airlines has been forced to follow this logic because customers have voted for cheap fares with their purse.

**

'This is the time to listen to frugal customers,' said Rags. 'One of the most successful real estate companies after the Great War offered young couples "dream homes" on paper. Only 600 sq. ft were built up. "Build the rest when you have money" was the popular, winning slogan.'

'In Bhutan being simple and frugal while being rich in happiness, is the rule rather than the exception,' I replied.

We took a tea break before taking the next quiz.

**

Dharmic Living

Your Dharmic Standards Assessment

Answer Yes (Y) / No (N)   Y   N

1. Do you stay away from judging the moral standards of others?
2. Do you feel any responsibility for the poor, crippled or sick?
3. Are your standards based on what your family practises?
4. Have you made your own decisions about what is honest and right?
5. Are honesty and integrity important to you in your family, with business partners and friends?
6. Do you avoid gossip?
7. Do you have a role in seeing that others are protected against unfairness or injustice?
8. Are you concerned with the quality of your family's life?
9. Do you treat others as you want to be treated?
10. Have you fought against injustice to others?

> Score
> Good: More than 7 Ys
> Adequate: Less than 5 Ys
> Poor: Less than 3 Ys

**

'I will follow all this when I am older,' I said flippantly.

'Are you sure you are destined to grow older?' asked Rags acidly.

I was stunned. Of course, no one knows.

'Be everything, do everything now,' he said. 'Who knows about tomorrow?'

We come up to a chasm yawning before us.

'Don't be afraid to jump,' said Rags. 'Remember, you can't cross a chasm in two small steps.' We jumped and landed safely.

He quoted the deaf, dumb and blind Helen Keller to me. 'Life is either a grand adventure or nothing. Security does not exist in Nature, nor do the children of men expect it. Avoiding danger is no safer in the long run than exposure.' She also said, 'Although the world is full of suffering, it is also full of overcoming it.'

'I sometimes fall in love with my own ideas. But I am afraid to actually implement them,' I said remembering all the times I had bitten my tongue before saying something really out of the box.

'The most important phrase in the English language is copyrighted by Nike: "Just do it!" Let it happen!'

'What happens if others laugh at me, if I fail, if I fall . . .?'

'Just get up and go again . . . that's all. Don't be afraid. People cannot discover new oceans till they have the courage to lose sight of the shore.'

We looked at some famous last words:

'Who the hell wants to hear actors talk?' Harry M. Warner, Warner Bros., 1927

'There is no likelihood. Man can never tap the power of

the atom.' Robert Millikan, awarded the Nobel Prize in Physics, 1923

'**Heavier than air flying machines are impossible.**' Lord Kelvin, President of the Royal Society, 1885

'"Another word for creativity is courage," wrote George Prince, founder of Synectics Inc.,' said Rags. 'Great inventions have grown only from impossible dream castles under which someone has built foundations. So follow your dreams. There are no guarantees. A ship in harbour is safe, a plane in the airport is safe. At home you are safe. But that is not why ships, aeroplanes or people were created— to be "safe". Look at all the people who stayed home and died in the Japanese earthquake!'

He handed me a new folder.

**

Future Consequences

Identify and forecast the various consequences of an action. You could identify the impact of a holiday resort in a forest. This could be:

- Improving the bottom line of the company
- Damaging the environment
- Harming the health of the employees

Sometimes the immediate impact on the company may be great, resulting in short-term profits. However, the long-term impact could be disastrous, creating many dissatisfied customers.

This is a forecasting tool which forces people to think of consequences in the following areas:

Consequences	1 month	6 month	1 year	5 years
Economic Consequences				
Social Consequences				
Environmental Consequences				
Political Consequences				
Emotional and Personal Consequences				

**

'If companies used this future consequences format, they would not do many of the things they do,' I said. 'The whole worldwide recession is the result of personal greed and a shortsighted view of profits.'

Rags handed me a questionnaire about workplaces.

**

Nurturing the Workplace

Your Workplace Wellness Assessment

Answer Yes (Y) / No (N)   Y   N

1. Would it be personally profitable for me to spend more time reading?
2. Do I effectively balance time between family, social, academic and recreational activities?
3. Do I concentrate too hard on just getting the job done rather than on my whole career?

4. Do I see my bosses as role models?
5. Do I hope that by improving my knowledge I will have a great career and a good life?
6. Are there some active steps I might take today to ensure a successful future?
7. Would talking to professionals in various fields help improve my job awareness?
8. Are there some channels, people or sources that could make this a pleasant experience?
9. Have I honestly assessed my potential for growth and participation in future jobs?
10. Do I travel for more than a week every month?
11. Do I rest when I am tired?
12. Have I learnt to say 'No' politely?

Score
Good: More than 9 Ys
Adequate: 5 or more Ys
Poor: Less than 5 Ys

**

'Why are people struggling to finish work and escape to their homes as quickly as they can? Is home the only place where they can really live?' asked Rags.

'That's not true. My friends and I have dinner at the company's expense and then leave for our shared flats,' I laughed.

'That's because you are a bachelor. Wait till you have a wife waiting for you at home.'

'Rima and I could meet for a romantic dinner and then go home,' I said dreamily.

*

Work–life balance is a broad concept including proper prioritizing between 'work' (career and ambition) on the one hand and 'life' (health, pleasure, leisure, family and spiritual development) on the other. Related, though broader, terms include 'lifestyle balance' and 'life balance'.

Although 64 per cent of workers feel that their work pressures are 'self-inflicted', they state that it is taking a toll on them. Additionally, men feel that there is a certain stigma associated with saying 'I can't do this'. To do more, one needs to move faster, to compete harder.

Increase in cardiovascular diseases, sexual health problems, a weaker immune system and frequent headaches, stiff muscles, or backaches are all the results of work pressure. It can also result in poor coping skills, irritability, jumpiness, insecurity, exhaustion and difficulty in concentrating. Stress may also perpetuate or lead to binge eating, smoking and alcohol consumption.

To get ahead, a seventy-hour work week is the new standard. What little time is left is often divided up among relationships, kids, and sleep. This increase in work hours over the past two decades means that less time will be spent with family, friends and community as well as in pursuing activities that one enjoys and taking the time to grow personally and spiritually. 90 per cent of working mothers and 95 per cent of working fathers report work–family conflicts. This affects happiness because it reduces the time available for quality time.

Research shows that the happiest subjects spent 70 per cent more time talking than the unhappiest subjects. Spending time with others is an index of happiness. Just adding five meaningful conversations to your weekly social calendar could boost your spirits dramatically.

*

'The time spent on the quest for power and status is time you cannot spend on other things, such as family. The price seems to be particularly severe for women,' said Rags.

'True. Many executive jobs require a substantial amount of overtime, which as a mother many cannot devote because of family obligations. Consequently, it is nearly impossible for a working mother in a top management position to be the primary caretaker of her child,' I said.

'According to sociologist Kathleen Gerson, young people are searching for new ways to define care that do not force them to choose between spending time with their children and earning an income and looking for definitions of personal identity that do not pit their own development against creating committed ties to others,' Rags said. 'Young adults believe that parents should get involved and support the children both economically and emotionally, as well as share labour equally. Young people do not believe work–life balance is possible and think it is dangerous to build a life dependent on another person when relationships are unpredictable. Whoever wants more—on the job, from the partner, from the children, from themselves—will one day be burnt out and empty inside. They are then faced with the realization that perfection does not exist. The burnout is the flip side of a successful career.'

'So we need better workplace policies, more flexi-time, vacation time, more celebrations, more community,' I noted.

HI

said the sms.

Hi!

I replied, while Rags smiled benignly at me.

Luv U

I shot off the sms before I could think too much.
A long silence.

AT LEAST LEARN TO SPELL THIS ONE THING

said her sms after two minutes. And the phone went dead.

'Really, you guys are too much. Why don't you settle this once and for all? You are old enough,' said Rags.

'Someone said to my friend Lokesh, "Aajkal shaadi email se hota hai!" And Lokesh said, "Email se hota hai? Maine socha shaadi female se hota hai!"'

'Really, it is time you wrote that perfect love letter with the proposal,' said Rags.

'Woof!' said Sirius. I hoped Coco, Rima's darling, would like him. She was a very fastidious Lhasa Apso with a shrill voice and a pedigree.

Rima once told me, 'If this dog was human, she would be too snobbish to talk to either of us!'

'Do you think she would be willing to get married in Bhutan?' I asked Rags.

'Ask her,' he said. 'Get the spellings right this time,' he added, looking thoroughly amused.

> **Will you marry me in Paro, Bhutan, on 16 November at 9 am?**

I smsed.

> **YES**

came the reply in a heartbeat.

I sat down on a rock to absorb the enormity of what I had done.

Rags was laughing his guts out and Sirius looked at us both with a baffled expression, with his tongue hanging out.

'Your having the wedding in Bhutan will contribute to the economic growth of this nation in the best possible way,' said Rags.

'Building roads with well-paid, free workers with good nutrition and medical facilities will build the economy,' he went on. 'Building them with half-starved workers threatened with violence is obviously not a good path to growth. The Bhutanese have religious festivals started by Zhabdung Ngawang Namgyal in the sixteenth century to "invoke happiness". The festivals last for three to five days and are celebrated with religious dances called *chhams* and elaborate ceremonies in all major dzongs. The local economy gets a real boost, with the people travelling across the country to attend and gain spiritual merit.'

'Every village temple has its "tiruvilla" in India, and the local people make a killing, thanks to the visitors,' I said.

'In India, we need to promote everything much more. Imagine if all these festivals had artists meeting to "earn a learning", to teach younger artists. We could use them to revive and teach temple arts,' Rags said.

'Dakshina Chitra in Chennai does it,' I remarked.

'Maybe we could reintroduce the devdasi system,' I said dreamily, remembering that Raja Raja Chola had 1550 devdasis in the big temple at Tanjore.

'For a fellow of thirty who has not even experienced a real kiss, you do talk a lot,' said Rags, dashing off downhill to escape my punch.

I was feeling like the *atsara* or clown in the Bhutanese festivals. These fellows work the crowd with their exaggerated gestures and irreverent jokes, creating the amusement needed to sit through the long-winded ceremonies.

Meanwhile, my heart was fluttering like a prayer flag and I hugged Sirius so hard that he ran away squeaking indignantly.

Should I ask her to bring Coco? No no, they may impound her, and never let her go!

Then we would have to spend the rest of our life in Bhutan—how blissful!

WHAT WILL I WEAR? I HAVE NOTHING TO WEAR

said Rima's text message, asking the eternal question of women through time.

I urged masterfully. Sirius looked adoringly at me as I
laughed loudly and scattered the pigeons that were peacefully
pecking away on a grassy mound.

Before me were the mountains that were full of temples
to Shiva and Parvati. Parvati, daughter of the mountain,
deserved the honour because she had wooed a bereaved
Shiva for over a thousand years. She had won him through
the power of her tapas. The Skanda Purana says, 'As the
sun dries the morning dew, so the sins of man dissipate at
the sight of the Himalayas.' But there were no Hindu temples
I could locate in Paro.

I handed Rags a poem I had written about Shiva when I
had gone hitchhiking in the Himalayas while still in college.

Indigo

Indigo, the sombre hue of storms,
Indigo mountains of forbidding hue,
Rise against a leaden stormy sky.
Still
With the stillness of the calm that falls
Before the dance of destruction.
Still as a yogi
Lost in the far pavilions of the mind.
Where coiled kundalini sleeps
Before it leaps.

The power
Of savage torrents of water
That fall
Into eternal nothingness

187

Over sharp sabre-toothed
Sentinel rocks.

The soundless shriek of winds
Imprisoned in the endless vaults of Time.

He is still,
Like a vast and starless sky,
Silent
Till the eternal bow snaps.
He wakes,
He who tames the torrent
With his locks.
Who makes the leaping tiger stop,
In mid-leap
And sets afire
The dark forbidding waves
Of a molten sea.

The immortal pulse of life is He,
Who makes
The atoms dance in cosmic dust
The rhythms of the universe flow
About his dance,
And blow
Around him
Until he stops
And stops the spinning universe
With his hypnotic gaze.

'This is a really good poem,' said Rags, looking at
me with genuine regard. 'Why don't you publish
your poems?'

'Oh, I have hundreds of them, but no one wants
to publish them. They want you to win the Nobel Prize

for Literature like Tagore before they will consider it,' I said despondently.

'Don't lose heart, keep writing. Write for the joy of it, write to record the voice of your Muse. When the world is ready to hear you, it will all happen,' said Rags comfortingly.

I wished I could do something fabulous and unforgettable for Rima.

Rags gave me a little bit of rolled parchment with the improvised wedding vows written on it.

It hit me then, what I should do to make our wedding unforgettable, something involving warriors and dances.

'Don't do it,' said Rags at once when he saw the wild look on my face.

'Why not?' I asked.

'It is in a Buddhist temple,' he said.

'So what?' I said, remembering that the white triangular prayer flags are supposed to carry the prayers of the faithful on the wings of the wind. I would buy both of us a prayer wheel with holy mantras on them. We would peacefully rotate them every day with our prayers, as we pecked away at our computers.

Rags was busy talking to the priest, who had come down to discuss the ceremony. We thought Rags could coach him. A beautiful synthesis of the Buddhist and Hindu ceremonies. The Lama listened patiently. He then said that he would stick to the Buddhist ceremony that he knew.

The wedding was to be at the Buddhist temple in Paro, Kyichu Lhakang.

Built in the seventh century by the Tibetan king Songsten Gampo, it was built as part of a plan to subdue an ogress who was lying across Tibet, Bhutan and the whole

Himalayan region, preventing the spread of Buddhism. The Kyichu Lhakang was built on her left foot along with 108 temples which were built on various parts of her body to prevent her from moving. The statue of Avalokiteswara with eleven heads and a thousand arms is a fine and venerated piece of art. In 1968 the Queen Mother had another temple constructed exactly like the older one. So well has the cultural heritage of Bhutan been preserved that it is hard to tell the difference between the two. The paintings on the walls include the Lord of the Four Directions, the murals of Buddha's sixteen early disciples and his twelve acts in previous reincarnations.

The priest Lama Tsherung was extremely supportive, he seemed to have conducted many weddings. He had been a monk since he was eleven years old and was now head of the small community of monks and nuns. The wedding would have fifteen nuns and priests chanting prayers for our long life and happiness. The whole wedding including breakfast and lunch for all would cost Rs 20,000. Sounded good to me. I went shopping with our driver Kandu to buy Rima's clothes: kira (an inner garment), tego and shawl. A lovely silver brooch completed my modest purchases.

My plans were clear. Rags, me and Sirius would meet her at the airport on the only flight on Druk Air at 11.30 a.m. I would gently seat her in a palanquin carried by four young Bhutanese. Rags and I would follow on mountain ponies. And the wedding would be the next day at 9.00 a.m., the auspicious time set by the priest.

Except that on that fateful day, there were no palanquins or bearers. They had never heard of such things in Bhutan. When Rima landed in a tee-shirt and jeans, she asked me, 'Where are my clothes?'

I handed her the traditional costume of the Bhutanese bride with matching silver jewellery. She handed over a gold mangalsutra which her mom had given her.

We arrived at the riverside resort in time for an exotic Bhutanese lunch. I sent Rima off for a hot stone bath followed by a massage at the spa. Rags assured me it was an ideal pre-wedding programme. Though how he knew about pre-wedding programmes, I didn't know. Rima disappeared for an early bedtime. I spent my last night as a bachelor treating myself and Sirius to a much needed bath.

Next morning, the four of us walked into the temple, with its fence of overgrown rose bushes and masses of red-gold marigolds. We walked past the elders turning the large red prayer wheels in the incense scented hallway. They smiled benignly at us: me and Rags in our new ghos and Rima, ravishing in her new kira. Sirius, freshly bathed and golden white, walked behind us, his plumed tail held aloft. We reached the courtyard where we were met by fifteen red-robed nuns and priests chanting mantras. Both of us were swathed in lovely white silk shawls in preparation for the ceremony.

Red chillies were drying in the courtyard. Trees laden with oranges stood witness in the corner.

The Lama firmly gestured for us to leave Sirius behind in the courtyard. 'Do you need to tie him up?' he asked in a whisper.

'No,' I whispered back indignantly.

'We'll both listen from outside,' said Rags.

Rima and I sat down on the floor at a low table in the sanctum, lit with butter lamps, and the ceremony began. The nuns and monks started chanting mantras in the cosy incense-suffused interior, full of tapestries, statues of Avalokiteswara and smelling of butter. The mantras surrounded and blanketed us in a soft tender peace.

After a couple of hours, we all went out to make our offerings to the old people outside. There was a metal altar to send up an invocations of smoke to the gods and a stupa to a renowed Lama. We shared our butter tea and a mouthful of rice and were declared married.

The monks and nuns ate a hearty meal with us and the wedding was over by noon. The prayers were for long life and happiness. We made no promises to each other.

We went back to the resort and Rags had a special surprise for us. He had invited his friend Somnath from the Hindu temple at Thimpu. The mangalsutra, the jayamala (made of roses) and the saptapadi followed.

The ceremony in the small hall, around the sacred fire, continued into the evening. After the sixth step of the saptapadi, I told Rima, 'You can still refuse to take the seventh step and the wedding is off.' She gave me a tough look—and with the next step, we were married to each other for seven lifetimes. The ceremony ended with sharing milk and sweet rice.

I kissed Sirius and hugged Rags. I didn't kiss or hug Rima. Rags looked pityingly at me. The look said, you have a long way to go . . .

It was time for us to go. 'Look, I don't think they will let you take Sirius through without a visa,' Somnath said. Sirius looked wistfully at us. I sat down on the ground and he gave me his matchless demonstration of unconditional love. I rubbed him down. Rima was crying and I was trying not to.

'Come, let's go,' called Rags. Sirius walked after him without a backward glance.

In my hand was a post-it slip he had given me. It read:

'For those who love each other, there is no separation in many lifetimes.'

It was time to move on.

Epilogue

Rima and I returned to our lives and began to practise the principles of happiness and the innovative thinking tools in our own lives.

Our happiness was infectious. We made many friends who got together to laugh, work, read and share. We planted more trees, cleaned up the roads, started walking and playing together with our kids. Knowledge, play, beauty and wisdom was shared. We created the village which is needed to raise a child in our little corner of Chennai. Garbage was used to make gardens and everything was bright and blooming. Now Anna Nagar has become one of many Shangri-Las in the world.

For Shangri-La is not really a place. It is within everyone's own heart. The dream city is only a reflection of our own peaceful, happy hearts. We realized that what the world needs today are small acts of kindness, gratitude and optimism, not some fantasy about returning to the lost Garden of Eden.

And Rags? He found many 'seeds' like me and Rima—bright, young, innovative and good. Rags is never tired, because he is always busy creating seeds for a better world. One seed at a time! I hear from him often on sms, on e-mail. I see him often in my dreams and hear his voice in my ear. But we have never met each other again.